GETTING STARTED

Before arriving, you need to plan out your day and get ready for the kids you will lead. Use the following steps for successful preparation.

PREPARE YOUR HEART

- ❏ Read the daily Scripture passages from your Bible (see the "Table of Contents" on page 2 for a complete list). Pray that God will speak to you through His Word.
- ❏ Read the "Leader Devotions" for each session (pages 8, 15, 22, 29, 36).
- ❏ Pray for the kids you will teach (page 4). Pray for yourself and the other leaders at VBS. Ask people to pray for you.

GET THE BASIC FACTS FROM YOUR VBS DIRECTOR

- ❏ Find out from your director how long you will have for Bible study each day. See below under "Plan" to determine how to plan your time.
- ❏ Find out how many kids to expect for your class.

PLAN

- ❏ Use these curriculum pieces:
  - This leader guide (one per teacher)
  - *VBS 2023 Grades 3–4 Bible Study Leader Pack* (9781087771724)—This pack includes a large banner, Bonus Verse posters, games, other fun teaching items, and a Music for Kids CD. (one per classroom)
  - *VBS 2023 Kids Activity Book* (9781087772080)—This fun book provides activities and tips to help kids engage in Bible study and gives them fun resources to take home at the end of the week. (one per kid)
- ❏ Read through the daily sessions. Highlight what you plan to include. Make notes of any changes or adjustments.
- ❏ The 30-minute Teach the Bible Study plan provides the core Bible teaching time. Additional Activity Options are included at the end of each session if your Bible study time is longer than 30 minutes, or if you will have two Bible study times (opening and closing).
- ❏ Make a supply list of the items you need.

GATHER AND PREPARE

- ❏ Sort and assemble items from your leader pack.
- ❏ Gather other supplies. (Some VBS directors will gather supplies for you. Check to be sure how your church does this.)

TEACH

- ❏ Relax and enjoy the chance to build relationships with your kids.
- ❏ Be flexible. Adjust your plans to make this the best experience possible for you and your kids.

CONTINUE THE CONNECTION

- ❏ Make sure your church has correct contact information for each child in your class.
- ❏ Keep the connection alive by looking for ways to stay connected with the kids you taught.

Send questions/comments to
VBS Publishing Team Leader by email to
rhonda.vancleave@lifeway.com
Or by mail to
VBS Publishing Team Leader
Grades 3–4 Bible Study Leader Guide
200 Powell Place, Suite 100
Brentwood, TN 37027-7707
or make comments on the
web at www.lifeway.com.

**EDITORIAL TEAM
KIDS MINISTRY PUBLISHING**

Chuck Peters
Director, Kids Ministry

Jeremy Carroll
*Publishing Manager,
VBS and Kids Discipleship*

Rhonda VanCleave
Publishing Team Leader

Bethany Phillips
Content Editor

Sara Lansford
Production Editor

Alli Quattlebaum
Graphic Designer

Beth McGill
Production Designer

Melissa Edgington
Writer

Melissa Edgington serves
in the children's ministry
at First Baptist Church in
Olney, Texas.

TABLE OF CONTENTS

TWISTS & TURNS™

Spin the spinner, beat the clock, skip ahead, level up, and play to win! You'll need to bring your A-game for this VBS! Twists & Turns is a fantastical celebration of games of all kinds. From classic tabletop games to strategy games to video games and more, kids will play their way through VBS in fun locations such as the Bible Study Game Room, Wild Card Crafts, Multi-player Missions, and Skip Ahead Snacks! But more importantly, they'll see Jesus through the eyes of one of His closest friends and discover that trusting Jesus as Savior and following Him changes the game entirely! Life is not all fun and games—even after becoming a Christian. It's full of twists and turns that can leave us feeling like we've taken one step forward and two steps back. That was certainly the case for Peter. He messed up; he stumbled; he wasn't perfect. But even when Peter messed up, it wasn't "Game Over." God still worked through Peter to help others learn about Jesus. As kids study five of Peter's encounters with Jesus, they'll discover that Jesus is holy, trustworthy, forgiving, worth following, and for everyone! Jesus guides us through all the twists and turns of our lives. He helps us know His ways and teaches us His paths. (Psalm 25:4) Following Jesus changes everything!

VBS MOTTO

Following Jesus changes everything.

LEVELS OF BIBLICAL LEARNING

People can obey Jesus as a response to His love.

CHRIST CONNECTION

Jesus changes everything. When we trust in Jesus as Savior and Lord, He forgives our sin and gives us new purpose. We can invite others to follow Him too.

VBS SCRIPTURE

Make your ways known to me, LORD; teach me your paths. *Psalm 25:4*

Shew me thy ways, O LORD; teach me thy paths. *Psalm 25:4 (KJV)*

DAY 1: JESUS IS HOLY

Peter Followed Jesus (Matthew 4:18-20; Luke 5:1-11)

Jesus sat in the boat of a fisherman named Peter to teach the crowds God's Word. Then, Jesus told Peter to take the boat into the deep water to catch fish. Peter said they had tried all night to catch fish, but he and the other fishermen obeyed Jesus. They caught so many fish their nets began to tear and break and their boats began to sink. When Peter saw this miracle he fell down at Jesus' feet. "Go away from me," Peter told Jesus, "because I am a sinful man, Lord!" Peter knew how sinful he was next to Jesus' holiness. "Don't be afraid," Jesus told Peter. "Follow Me, and I will make you fish for people." Peter and the other fishermen left everything and followed Jesus.

DAY 2: JESUS IS TRUSTWORTHY

Peter Walked to Jesus on the Water (Matthew 14:22-33)

Jesus told His disciples to go ahead of Him in a boat. The disciples' boat was far from shore. The wind and water grew rough. The disciples saw Jesus walking on top of the water toward them. Peter asked to walk to Jesus on the water, and Jesus said, "Come." Peter noticed how strong the wind was and got scared. He began to sink and cried out, "Lord, save me!" Jesus saved him. Jesus asked Peter, "Why did you doubt Me? Is your faith really so small?" As soon as Jesus and Peter got back into the boat, the wind stopped! The disciples worshiped Jesus and said, "It's true. You really are the Son of God!"

DAY 3: JESUS IS FORGIVING

Peter Denied Jesus and Was Restored (Luke 22:31-34,54-62; John 18:15-18; 21:1-19)

Jesus told Peter that before the day was over Peter would deny he knew Jesus three different times. That night, soldiers arrested Jesus. During Jesus' trial, Peter sat nearby. Three different times, Peter denied knowing Jesus. The next day, Jesus was crucified. His body was buried. On the third day, Jesus rose from the dead!

Some time later Peter and a few disciples decided to go fishing. They caught nothing. A man on the shore suggested they put the net on the right side of the boat. They did and caught 153 fish! They realized the man was Jesus! Jesus shared bread and fish with them on the shore. Jesus asked Peter, "Do you love Me?" three different times. Peter replied, "Yes, Lord, You know I love You." Jesus told Peter to take care of the other followers of Jesus.

DAY 4: JESUS IS WORTH FOLLOWING

Peter Spoke Boldly about Jesus (Acts 3:1–4:24)

As Peter and John were going to the temple, they saw a man who couldn't walk. Peter healed the man through Jesus' power. People who knew the man were amazed, and Peter taught them the good news about how Jesus died and rose again to save people from their sins. The religious leaders were annoyed that Peter and John were preaching about Jesus. They arrested the two disciples. The next day, Peter and John stood before the religious leaders and spoke boldly about Jesus. The leaders knew these uneducated men could speak this way because they had been with Jesus. The leaders commanded the disciples not to teach about Jesus anymore. Peter and John said, "We can't stop." They knew they had to tell people about Jesus no matter what happened.

DAY 5: JESUS IS FOR EVERYONE

Peter Told Cornelius About Jesus (Acts 10)

Cornelius was a Roman officer who worshiped God. One afternoon an angel of God appeared in a vision and told Cornelius to send men to Joppa and find a man named Peter. Cornelius obeyed. Meanwhile, Peter had a vision. The vision was about unclean animals. A voice told Peter not to call something unclean if God had made it clean. Peter was trying to understand the vision when the men looking for him arrived. The Holy Spirit told Peter to go with the men. Cornelius, his family, and friends were waiting to hear Peter's message. Peter said, "God has shown me that He does not show favoritism. Every person can be right or acceptable to God through faith in Him." Peter taught that everyone who believes in Jesus will have their sins forgiven. Everyone who heard the message became believers.

CHARACTERISTICS OF THIRD AND FOURTH GRADERS

During VBS, kids have the opportunity to see how a personal relationship with Jesus Christ is crucial. They can learn that they can trust Jesus every step of the way. To help you lead kids of this age begin and grow their relationship with Jesus, here are a few things to keep in mind.

PHYSICALLY AND SOCIALLY

are active, energetic, and enthusiastic by nature and need an outlet for those physical characteristics with active learning experiences

are in the process of building relationships, usually loyal to their friends (generally of the same gender) and want to be helpful to the group or team

like to work in groups and focus on fairness

do not want to call attention to themselves or be compared to others; They are more comfortable playing a game or answering questions as part of a group.

are beginning to take more responsibility for their actions

SPIRITUALLY

are developing values and thinking in terms of right or wrong instead of good and bad

are learning that the Bible tells of God's plan of salvation

can memorize short Bible passages and learn and apply Bible truths about salvation

can ask serious questions about faith and religion

can follow the examples, teachings, and commandments of Jesus

are aware that God loves and values all people

EMOTIONALLY

are increasing in their self concept

can be strong-willed at times as they seek ways to show independence

can be anxious, withdrawn, tend to complain, and are often hesitant to try new activities

are generally sensitive, their feelings are hurt easily, and they cry easily

BIBLE SKILLS

are able to locate some books in the Bible

can locate books of the Bible by using the contents page or with a leader's assistance

can find information asked for by reading a verse or passage

can pronounce some of the names of Bible people, places, and things

can discover and apply truths in a Bible passage

learn that Bible truths never change

begin to use the Bible for daily Bible reading

know the Bible teaches people how God wants them to live

TEACHING TIP

To become more familiar with third and fourth graders, consider watching television programming aimed at this age group, visiting the children's section of a bookstore, and walking down the toy aisles of a local department store. Ask kids you know what social media influencers they are following and what video games they are playing as well.

TIPS FOR GUIDING BEHAVIOR

PREVENTION IS THE PREFERRED STRATEGY

When it comes to classroom management, I'd rather prevent a problem than deal with a problem. That, over the years, has become my stance. In other words, if it is at all possible to prevent a behavior issue, that's the route I'd prefer to take.

I believe that most children want to please the adults in their lives. However, consistently we hear that classroom management is one of the top issues faced by kids ministry leaders today. I think we have to look at the root of the problem—Why is the child acting out? What is it that would cause him to consistently misbehave?

THE WHYS OF POOR BEHAVIOR

Understanding the "why" behind misbehavior can help us know the systems to put in place that allow kids to be successful and thus prevent the poor behavior. This strategy takes time, effort, and energy, but it's worth it! Again, I'd rather work to prevent poor behavior than to deal with it. Consider some of these "whys" for poor behavior:

- Need for more attention—There are a variety of reasons that some children need more attention than others. At times they will do whatever it takes to get it. Giving extra attention to these children can prevent outbursts and actions that fill their needs in negative ways.
- Masking insecurity—The class clown may prefer to be laughed with than laughed at. Be careful not to create situations where this child chooses to hide his lack of knowledge (or maybe even his lack of ability to share knowledge) by acting out. Remember, look past the actions and look for the cause.
- Find it hard to manage their anger—Kids who "blow up" and are quick to "fight" may not have the skills to avoid these outbursts. Watch for opportunities to head off the poor behavior and give a child the chance to cool down and self-correct.
- Looking for ways to be in control—Some kids feel more secure when they are in control. They want to be the teacher and look for ways to fulfill that desire, even if it means disrupting the teacher's plans. Remember that the very thing that irritates you most about these children may be the very thing God wants to use for their success. Look past the arrogance of their behavior and choose to foster their leadership potential.
- Full of energy—Most kids I know are full of energy. It's the way God created them and is part of His plan to help them develop. Unfortunately, many teachers ignore that fact and attempt to suppress their energy instead of joining God in His plan. It's been said that a child has an approximate one-minute attention span for every year old she is. Asking a four-year-old to sit still and listen for ten minutes goes against how she was created. Don't fight it; join it! Look for opportunities to include movement in your sessions. Move away from the tables and chairs and let the kids move!
- Boredom—When a child gets bored (or thinks he's bored) he starts looking for something to do. Most of the time it doesn't include the session teaching aim. Some kids get bored easier than others and teachers need to be ready. Plan sessions that consider the children, their preferences, and their abilities. More often than not, behavior issues can be connected to the sessions we plan or fail to plan (ouch).

MAKE BEHAVIOR EXPECTATIONS UNDERSTOOD

Often, kids don't live up to our expectations because they don't know what we expect. Make sure your behavior expectations are understood. If you have kids who don't understand their behavior is wrong, they won't know how to prevent poor behavior. Don't make a mile long list of rules, but share that respect for each other is mandatory. That really covers most issues.

At the end of the day, behavior is all about knowing and understanding the kids you teach. Read and discover general characteristics, try to learn as much as you can about the kids you will be teaching, then put systems in place that will allow for success. Consider the why and then create a solution.

Bill Emeott is the Minister to Children at Houston's First Baptist Church. He is a graduate of Clayton State University, Mercer University, and New Orleans Baptist Theological Seminary.

DECORATING THE BIBLE STUDY GAME ROOM

The Bible Study Game Room is a place for kids to gather and dig deeper into the Bible study and build relationships.

FOCAL WALL SUGGESTIONS

- As you determine how to set up your Bible study area, you may want to select one wall as your focal wall to display teaching items from the *VBS 2023 Grades 3–4 Bible Study Leader Pack* (9781087771724). Keeping the focal wall simple with only teaching items only will help eliminate distractions while teaching biblical truths.
- Display the "Twists & Turns Banner" (item 1) throughout the week and add the "Twists & Turns Banner Add-ons" (item 2) each day.
- Prepare to change out the remaining pack items as they are called for each day.

ACTIVITY-BASED DECORATION

- Create a child-size gameboard path across your floor, or on the wall on butcher paper, using painter's or masking tape. Or create board game spaces with pieces of construction paper and attach using tape or clear contact plastic. Include instructions such as *Go forward 2, Go back 3, Hop in place until the next person rolls,* and so forth.
- Consider adding the *VBS 2023 Floor Prints* (9781087776743), which are designed to create a bright, colorful gameboard path! Make kids feel like they are inside a board game!
- Use the *VBS 2023 Giant Inflatable Game Cube* (9781087779812) and the accompanying download to create a die.
- Play the game you've created with kids who arrive early or leave late or if you need to fill a few extra minutes during your schedule. Let kids be the game pieces if your game is on the floor or use sticky notes as game pieces if you used the wall. There are suggestions for using this path as part of your Bible study time throughout this leader guide.

FUN OPTIONS FOR OTHER AREAS OF THE ROOM

- Display a *VBS 2023 Bible Study Location Sign* (9781087776811) outside the room. Add punch-outs from the *VBS 2023 Wall Art* (9781087776729) around the sign.
- Attach the *VBS 2023 Supersized Backdrop* (9781087776699) to one wall to help create the Bible Study Game Room.
- Scatter beanbag chairs and other comfortable seating around your teaching area.
- Fill bookshelves with board games, teaching supplies, and other fun items you might find in a game room.
- Include low tables; new, clean galvanized drip pans; and other large flat surfaces in your room so that you are ready to play some games! Large and small pans allow you to put games away without losing your place if you need to come back to something.
- Find additional decorating ideas in the *VBS 2023 Decorating Made Easy* book (9781087772110).
- Hang *VBS 2023 Visual Pack* (9781087776736) posters on other classroom walls.
- Drape *VBS 2023 String Flags* (9781087776750) and *VBS 2023 Whirleys* (9781087776804) from the ceiling.
- Use small containers or *VBS 2023 Cups* (9781087776460) to hold pens and supplies.

VBS 2023 Decorating Made Easy

VBS 2023 Supersized Backdrop

CONTINUE VBS AT HOME

Research shows the important opportunities VBS gives adults to connect with and invest in kids and families. (You can read more about the research yourself in *It's Worth It: Uncovering How One Week Can Transform Your Church*, 9781535952736.) You've spent this week intentionally investing in the kids in your class! So how do you continue connecting with kids after VBS is over?

There's no one right way to do this, but a few ideas include greeting kids in the hallways at church, volunteering with your church's ongoing kids ministry, and participating in your church's follow-up efforts so you can build relationships with kids and their families. Be on the lookout for times these families go through twists and turns in life and be there to support them, along with your church body.

At the end of VBS, you may also consider writing a note to each kid in your class on a *VBS 2023 Note Card* (9781087776507) or *Postcard* (9781087776880). Tell kids what you're praying for them, and call out gifts you see that God has given them. Remind them that God has a special plan for their lives.

Below are several resources that can be paired with your note to send the VBS content home with kids. Kids can use these resources independently or with their parents. Encourage kids to use these resources to share the gospel with friends and family members.

VBS 2023 Kids Activity Book (9781087772080)—Whether or not you used this during VBS, send a copy home with the kids! This book is filled with fun games and activities. Kids will also find a Bible story summary, Bible verse references, and information about the gospel. Encourage kids to use this to engage with the VBS Bible content for themselves.

*VBS 2023 Memory Make*r (9781087776545) These six tags help kids follow along during the Bible study time. Even more important, the tags help kids make a memory they can take home with them. This year, kids and preschoolers will use the same tags, adding them to a muslin bag each day, along with other keepsakes collected during VBS. Kids can carry home memory makers to share Bible content and fun memories with family and friends.

VBS 2023 Parent Guide (9781087777061)—This is a tool for parents to use with their kids. This year's guide includes a VBS themed board game on one side and a set of family devotions on the other. Family devotions will help parents and kids read God's Word together, while spending time connecting as a family.

VBS 2023 Suction Cup Spinner (9781087776620)—If you've ever made your own spinner with a brad and a paper clip, you're going to love this! Families can use this with the game on one side of the *VBS 2023 Parent Guide* to play more seamlessly, as well as using it with any other games they may own.

VBS 2023 Devotional Bible for Kids CSB or KJV (9781087783536 or 9781087783543)—This is a great way to ensure that kids have a Bible at home. An added bonus is that this Bible has 30 devotions to help kids start having a quiet time.

Twists & Turns Devotional (9781087777719)—Sudden sadness, confusing fear, surprising joy. Do you feel like life is full of the unexpected? You're not alone! In these one hundred short devotions and activities, kids will travel the winding roads of the apostle Peter's life and ministry. Peter had to learn that Jesus was with him always, and this devotional will help kids do the same as they learn to trust God through every twist and turn.

VBS 2023 Music for Kids CD (9781087772646)—This CD has the VBS theme song "Twists & Turns" as well as daily songs that go with the five days of VBS. Kids will learn the music during Bible study, Worship Rally, and Music Rotation and will love having a CD of their own to share with their families!

DAY 1: JESUS IS HOLY

BIBLE STORY

Peter Followed Jesus (Matthew 4:18-20; Luke 5:1-11)

TODAY'S POINT

Jesus is holy and that changes everything!

BIBLE VERSE

Make your ways known to me, LORD; teach me your paths. *Psalm 25:4*

Shew me thy ways, O LORD; teach me thy paths. *Psalm 25:4 (KJV)*

LEADER DEVOTION

Have you ever followed a map or road sign, confident of the directions, only to be turned onto a road where you never intended to go? If so, you likely felt frustrated. There are times in all our lives that we can look back and remember with certainty a path or direction in life that we were following with confidence, only to be derailed by an unexpected encounter.

In today's Bible story we meet Peter, a fisherman by trade who probably had very clear expectations of his path and direction in life. One day, Peter had been fishing all night and was washing his nets near the shore where Jesus was teaching crowds of people. Perhaps Peter was listening to Jesus with curiosity at a distance as he cleaned his nets, unaware of the twist he was about to encounter.

After teaching the crowds from a boat that belonged to Peter, Jesus turned to Peter and asked him to go out to catch fish. Peter responded that they had fished all night and caught nothing. Yet, at Jesus' request, Peter obeyed, and he caught more fish than he could have ever imagined.

"When Simon Peter saw this, he fell at Jesus's knees and said, 'Go away from me, because I'm a sinful man, Lord!'" (Luke 5:8)

Peter sank to his knees in repentance and worship, recognizing that this miracle of fish was something only someone with God's power could do. Encountering Jesus changes everything.

This week, you will introduce kids to Jesus, perhaps for the very first time. Some of the kids you encounter will be new and curious about who this Jesus is, like the crowds on the shoreline. Some may be listening more intently, questioning if this Jesus is worth following. You will meet kids who are beginning to understand foundational truths about Jesus. Others will have already believed and trusted in Jesus and are taking their first steps toward growing in their faith. No matter where the kids you teach are in their spiritual journeys, Jesus has something to teach them this week about who He is—and He is going to use you to help kids encounter Him.

As you prepare to lead, ask God to speak His truth through you, so children may encounter Jesus as Peter did, recognizing that He is truly the Son of God. As we will learn this week, Peter's life did not come without twists and turns along the way. Nevertheless, Peter followed because he met Jesus, and that changed everything.

REFLECT

- What twists and turns in your life have brought you to where you are today?
- Think about circumstances that have helped you know who Jesus truly is. What have you learned?
- How can you help the kids you teach know that Jesus is real and that He loves them?

NOTES

START IT PREP

- ❑ Pack items 1 and 2
- ❑ Various game pieces
- ❑ Paper sack
- ❑ Colored paper
- ❑ Clear contact plastic
- ❑ *VBS 2023 Giant Inflatable Game Cube* (9781087779812)
  - Download and print the number inserts that came with the cube, or write the numbers *1–6* on pieces of paper. Place the number inserts in the *Giant Inflatable Game Cube.*
  - Gather game pieces from various games. Place them inside a paper sack.
  - Make gameboard "spaces" on the floor using colored paper and clear contact plastic. Use the spaces to create a focused seating area for kids during Bible study time.
  - Display the "Twists & Turns Banner" (item 1) on the focal wall. Cut apart "Twists & Turns Add-ons" (item 2) to use each day.

START IT TIPS

- Use hula hoops or *VBS 2023 Floor Prints* (9781087776743) to create gameboard spaces instead.
- Gather game pieces from old games at yard sales or purchase online in bulk so that you can allow kids to put the pieces in their memory maker bags during "Finish It" as a reminder of VBS.

LEARN IT PREP

- ❑ Pack item 3
- ❑ Bible
- ❑ Game pieces from "Start It"
  - Display the "Day 1 Bible Story Picture" (item 3) on a focal wall, or place near your Bible to hold up as you tell the story.

START IT (5 MINUTES)

1. Welcome kids as they enter the room and direct them to stick their hands into the bag of game pieces and choose one. Guide kids to roll the game cube to determine how far to move along the path before sitting down on an empty space.

2. Say: "Welcome to Twists & Turns, where following Jesus changes the game! I am so excited that you're here to play games and learn with me at VBS this week!"

3. Invite the kids to show their game pieces to the people sitting near them and share what their favorite games are.

4. Ask: "Why do you think we like games so much?" *(They're fun; They're funny; We like winning, and so forth)*

5. Say: "One great thing about games is the way everything can change so quickly! All kinds of twists and turns come up, and unexpected things happen, both good and bad! Games are kind of like life in that way. We never know exactly what's going to happen on any given day, do we?"

6. Explain that Peter is a real, historical person we can read about in the Bible and a really surprising thing happened to him one day. He was just going along, living his regular life. Suddenly, he met Jesus, and that changed everything!

7. Show the kids the "Twists & Turns Banner" (item 1). Add the Day 1 "Banner Add-on" (item 2). Guide a volunteer to read the caption aloud.

8. Say: "In today's story from the Bible, Peter begins to learn that Jesus is holy. That means Jesus is different from anything or anyone else. There's no one like Jesus. And once Peter learned that, everything was different."

LEARN IT (12 MINUTES)

1. Say: "Before we hear the story, I want to play a little game. I'm going to name some things that someone can do. If I name something that you, a kid, can do, I want you to hold your game piece to your chest. If it's something only a grownup can do, hold your game piece out toward me. And if it's something that no one but God can do, hold your piece up in the air."

2. Name the following actions, pausing after each one to let the kids decide what to do with their game pieces: driving to the grocery store, paying bills, picking up toys, creating the world, taking a spelling test, going to work at an office, making it snow, playing a video game, and buying a house.

3. Display the "Day 1 Bible Story Picture" (item 3) and show kids the fishing net.

4. Say: "In today's Bible story, we will learn about Peter's encounter with Jesus. Peter saw Jesus do a miracle. A *miracle* is something amazing that only God can do. Listen for the miracle, and when you think you hear it, hold your game piece high in the air."

5. Open your Bible to Matthew 4. Tell the Bible story. The story has been provided for you to use as a guide.

PETER FOLLOWED JESUS

Jesus had been teaching large crowds of people about the kingdom of God. While Jesus was standing on the shore of the Sea of Galilee, the crowds began pressing in to hear God's Word. Jesus noticed two boats at the edge of the lake. Some fishermen had left their boats on the shore and were washing their nets from fishing the night before. Jesus got into the boat that belonged to Peter. Jesus asked Peter to take the boat into the water a short distance from the shore. Jesus sat down in the boat and continued teaching the crowds.

After teaching the people, Jesus turned to Peter. "Take the boat out into the deep water and let down your nets to catch fish." Peter answered Jesus. "Master, we worked hard all night to catch fish, and we did not catch anything. But if You say so, I will let down the nets."

Peter and the other fishermen obeyed Jesus. They took their boat into the deep water and let down their nets to catch fish. When they did, they caught so many fish that their nets began to tear and break. The fishermen were amazed! They signaled for the other fishermen along the shore to come help them. The men filled both boats with so much fish that the boats started to sink. When Peter saw this miracle, he recognized that Jesus is holy.

Peter fell down at Jesus' feet. "Go away from me," Peter told Jesus, "because I am a sinful man, Lord!" Peter knew how sinful he was next to Jesus' holiness.

"Don't be afraid," Jesus told Peter. "Follow Me, and I will make you fish for people." Peter and the other fishermen brought the boats to shore, left everything, and followed Jesus.

Jesus' miracle demonstrated that He is Lord of everything, including the sea and everything in it. Peter saw the fish and knew that this miracle was something only God could do. He recognized that Jesus is holy and has power that comes from God alone. Peter was just beginning to understand who Jesus really is.

Matthew 4:18-20; Luke 5:1-11

1. Ask: "What was the miracle that Jesus did?" *(He caused the fishermen to catch more fish than their nets could even hold.)*
2. Ask: "What was Peter's reaction when he saw this miracle?" *(He fell down at Jesus' feet and called himself a sinful man.)*
3. ✝ Say: "When Jesus did this miracle, He was showing Peter and the others that He is God. God is holy, which means He is completely different from anyone or anything else. When Peter saw that Jesus is holy, he recognized how different Jesus is. Peter fell at Jesus' feet because Peter knew he was a sinner, and Jesus is perfect because Jesus is God the Son! Being sinful means that you do wrong things. We're all sinful! Peter knew that sin separates us from God. We're going to learn this week how Jesus came so we can have forgiveness for our sins and have a relationship with Him! We'll also get to see Peter's relationship with Jesus grow and change over time."

HELPFUL DEFINITION
Holy—to be separate; holy describes God's character as totally unique and separate from what He created. Sin separates us from God.

SHARING THE GOSPEL
The ✝ identifies an opportune time to share the gospel as led by the Holy Spirit.

KNOW IT PREP
- [ ] Pack item 4
- [ ] Plastic box
- [ ] Large fish stuffed animal
- [ ] Game pieces from "Start It"
  - Display the "Theme Verse Poster" (item 4) on a focal wall.

LEADER TIP
Allow the fish stuffed animal to become your classroom mascot for the week! Kids can take turns carrying the fish up and down the halls and repeat the game each day to learn the verse!

LIVE IT PREP
- [ ] *VBS 2023 Kids Activity Books*
- [ ] Pencils

FINISH IT PREP
- [ ] *VBS 2023 Memory Makers* and Day 1 tags
- [ ] Game pieces from "Start It" if you will be allowing kids to keep them
- [ ] Basket to hold Memory Makers each day (optional)

KNOW IT (5 MINUTES)

1. Choose a leader to do different motions with his game piece. For instance, he may put it on his head or set it on the floor and walk in a circle around it. Guide the other kids to follow the leader, mimicking his actions.
2. Read the "Theme Verse Poster" (pack item 4) aloud together.
3. Say: "In today's story, Jesus showed us that He is God. He's a good leader! He will lead us down the right paths so that we can follow Him the way Peter did."
4. Talk about how Peter immediately left his fishing nets and followed Jesus.
5. Guide kids to sit in a circle. Explain that the person you give the fish stuffed animal to will say the first word of Psalm 25:4 aloud and then toss the fish to someone else in the circle. That person will say the next word and toss the fish again. Continue until the whole verse has been said several times.
6. If kids are doing well at remembering the verse, guide a leader to stand in front of the "Theme Verse Poster" (item 4) and see if kids can play the game without looking.

LIVE IT (5 MINUTES)

1. Give kids activity books and pencils. Allow them to write their names on inside front covers.
2. Guide kids to find the Bible story on page 2. Ask volunteers to share one thing they remember about today's story.
3. Say: "We learned today that Jesus is holy! Let's do the maze on page 3 to help us remember what holy means." *(Jesus is completely perfect and set apart from everything else.)*
4. Explain that the leftover words after they do the maze will give the answer to the funny riddle. (Why are cats so good at video games? *Because they have nine lives.*)
5. Guide kids to turn to 1 Peter 1:15-16 and ask a volunteer to read the verses aloud. Discuss the Level Up! question on page 3 as time allows.

FINISH IT (3 MINUTES)

1. Give each child a Day 1 tag and a Logo tag to add to her Memory Maker bag, as well as a game piece if kids will be keeping those.
2. Ask for a volunteer to tell you what icon is on the Day 1 tag *(a fish)*. Ask another volunteer to read the words on the reverse side *(Jesus Is Holy)*. Ask kids how either side will remind them of what they learned from today's Bible story. Allow some time to discuss.
3. Gather the kids' Memory Makers to save until tomorrow.
4. Encourage the kids to share with someone at home what it means that Jesus is holy.
5. Pray for kids, asking God to help them follow Jesus the way Peter did.

JESUS EQUALS PERFECTION

(Application Activity #1—10 minutes)

- ❏ Pack items 5 and 6
- ❏ Scissors
- ❏ Paper clips
- ❏ Timer
- • Make enough copies of the "Jesus Equals Perfection Grid" (item 5) and "Jesus Equals Perfection Game Pieces" (item 6) for several teams. Cut apart the game pieces and clip each set together.

1. Say: "Today we've been learning about what it means for Jesus to be holy. Peter saw Jesus' holiness in today's story."

2. Ask a volunteer to share what he's learned about Jesus' holiness. *(Jesus is different from anyone. Jesus is perfect. Jesus is God.)*

3. Group the kids into teams. Give each team a "Jesus Equals Perfection Grid" and set of game pieces (pack items 5 and 6).

4. Explain that the kids will have one minute to work as a team to perfectly match up the pieces with the spaces on the grid.

5. When the timer buzzes, talk about how easy or difficult it was to perfectly fill in the grid.

6. Say: "We can't be perfect like Jesus. We are all sinners—we do wrong things. But Jesus can help us be more like Him! We can learn more about Jesus the way Peter did."

7. Point out the fish and boat symbols on the grid and ask the kids to recall what each one has to do with today's story. Allow kids to make any other connections they see as time allows.

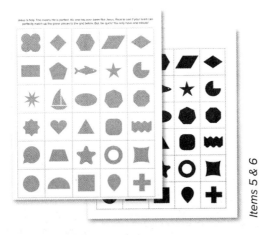

Items 5 & 6

FISHING FOR PEOPLE

(Application Activity #2—10 minutes)

- ❏ No supplies needed

1. Ask: "What miracle did Jesus perform in today's story?" *(He caused the fishermen to catch so many fish their nets couldn't hold them all.)*

2. Say: "After the men caught all of those fish, Jesus told Peter that if he would follow Jesus, Jesus would make him someone who fishes for people instead of fish."

3. Explain that Jesus was asking Peter to come with Him and help other people see who Jesus really is. Jesus wanted Peter to be someone who helped tell others that Jesus is holy and that Jesus is God the Son! In other words, He wanted Peter to help draw more people near to Jesus so they could choose to follow Jesus. So Peter followed Jesus and helped tell others about Him.

4. Say that you will play a fishing game to remind kids of what Peter did for a living before he began to follow Jesus. Choose one child to be the fisherman and stand in the middle of the room. Guide all of the other kids to line up on the wall on one end of the room.

5. Explain that the fisherman will give instructions to the "fish." For instance, if the fisherman says, "Tiptoe, little fish!" All of the kids will tiptoe from one side of the room to the other. (Other ideas include: run, swim, skip, crawl, hop, and so forth.)

6. Instruct fishermen to say, "Lower the net!" at various points during the game when the fish are halfway across the room. The kids must link arms with a partner. Meanwhile, the fisherman will tag as many kids as he can before they find partners.

7. Guide kids who get tagged to join the fisherman in the center, catching fish.

NEW TESTAMENT CONNECTION

(Bible Skills Activity—10 minutes)

- ❑ Pack item 7
- ❑ Bibles (1 per kid)
- ❑ Sticky notes in two colors (1½ by 2 inches or similar)
- • Place the "New Testament Connection" gameboard (item 7) on a playing surface.

1. Group the kids into two teams and give each child a Bible. Show kids the table of contents at the front of their Bibles.

2. Say: "The Bible is divided into two main parts: the Old Testament and the New Testament. Today's story is found in the New Testament. The New Testament starts with the news that Jesus is about to be born. It's the part of the Bible where we read about Jesus' birth and His life."

3. Point out that the Bible is made up of 66 different books. Explain that they can use the table of contents to help them find different books in the Bible. For example, today's story is in the book of Matthew. Challenge the kids to use the table of contents to locate Matthew in their Bibles.

4. Give each team a pad of sticky notes. Each team should have a different color. Display "New Testament Connection" (item 7).

5. Explain that the teams are going to race to see who can place four sticky notes in a row, in any direction, on the poster. Their teams will get a chance to place a sticky note if they are the first to locate the New Testament book that you call out. Point out that in this game, part of the strategy is blocking the other team on the gameboard.

6. The first team to get four in a row wins!

Item 7

FISH FINDER

(Bonus Verse Activity—10 minutes)

- ❑ Pack items 8 and 9
- ❑ Scissors
- • Display the "Day 1 Bonus Verse Poster: Acts 2:21" (item 8) on a focal wall.
- • Cut apart the "Fish Finder" cards (item 9). Write the words of the Bible verse and reference beneath the fish (one word or phrase per fish) in the translation of your choice.

1. Read the bonus verse poster (item 8) together.

2. ✝ Say: "When Peter fell at Jesus' feet, Jesus told Peter to follow Him. Jesus welcomes anyone who calls on His name and admits that he or she is a sinner. He promises that He will rescue us from our sins if we repent and trust in Him. We'll learn more about what being a Christian and following Jesus means as we study the Bible this week."

3. Shuffle and lay out the "Fish Finder" cards facedown on the floor.

4. Let the kids take turns turning over two cards at a time to try to find matching fish. If they turn over a matching pair, guide them to set it aside.

5. After all of the matching fish have been found, lead the kids to put the words of the Bible verse together in order.

Item 9

DAY 2: JESUS IS TRUSTWORTHY

BIBLE STORY

Peter Walked to Jesus on the Water (Matthew 14:22-33)

TODAY'S POINT

Jesus is trustworthy even when I doubt.

BIBLE VERSE

Make your ways known to me, LORD; teach me your paths. *Psalm 25:4*

Shew me thy ways, O LORD; teach me thy paths. *Psalm 25:4 (KJV)*

LEADER DEVOTION

Immediately. A word I've passed over time and time again in this passage, yet one that stuck out to me as I read it this time. And then, I couldn't stop seeing it!

In fact, the Day 2 passage begins with it. "Immediately he made the disciples get into the boat and go ahead of him to the other side, while he dismissed the crowds." Intrigued, I decided to find out what Jesus had been doing prior to this. It seems like this was a busy day for Jesus and the disciples. They had just fed five thousand men plus their families with only five loaves and two fish! So, when Jesus told them to get in the boat while He dismissed the crowds, I'm thinking they were exhausted and happy to oblige.

What I'm pondering, though, is why immediately? I know God's timing is perfect—but why in such a hurry? Was it because Jesus wanted to be alone to talk with the Father? Maybe. Or could it be that He knew just when that storm was going to hit and exactly when the disciples needed to leave so they could see and experience this miracle? Maybe both!

The next time we see our word for the day it is more dramatic. The wind was blowing furiously, and the waves were crashing against the boat. A boat—not a ship! The disciples were terrified because in addition to the wind and the waves, they thought they saw a ghost! But here it is again: "Immediately Jesus spoke to them. 'Have courage! It is I. Don't be afraid.'" (Matthew 14:27) Jesus was quick to comfort. I love that. He knew exactly what they needed to hear to alleviate at least part of their fear. I picture a child crying out in fear of a monster under her bed. Dad hears her cry, steps into the darkened room, and the fear subsides. Sometimes just knowing someone bigger and stronger is with you makes you feel better—even though the "supposed danger" is still there.

Peter, being "blown away" by what he was seeing, asked to join in! Jesus said, "Come," so Peter climbed out of the boat. (By the way, it looks as if this happened immediately as well. We don't read that Peter asked again. I think we need to credit Peter, who didn't hesitate when he was called.) Peter began walking toward Jesus. Unfortunately, that's when Peter took his focus off Jesus and focused on the storm surrounding him instead. Just as we often do, Peter began to sink, but Jesus immediately reached out His hand and rescued Peter.

Jesus could have calmed the storm while He was walking on the sea or when Peter got out of the boat. He could have calmed the storm as His hand caught Peter's. But He didn't. Instead, He walked through the storm with Peter. You might think that was enough. But still, there was more the disciples had to learn.

When Jesus and Peter got into the boat, the wind ceased. This is when the disciples finally said, "Truly you are the Son of God." It was neither when He walked on the water nor when He rescued Peter, but it was when He quieted the storm they were going through. The disciples seemed to miss everything else that had just happened right in front of their eyes before they declared it!

I don't know about you, but when I'm waiting for the miracle I want to see, I often fail to notice all the miracles in the background. My prayer for you and for me is that we'll take notice of all that God is doing around us and know that truly, Jesus is the Son of God and that He changes everything!

REFLECT

- Peter did not wait for the storm to stop before getting out of the boat. What are you hesitant about doing that God has called you to do?
- When Peter focused on the storm instead of Jesus, he was scared. Who or what are you focusing on?
- Jesus didn't stop the storm immediately. He walked through it with Peter. What are storms you see kids facing now? How can you help them know that they are not alone, that Jesus is walking with them?

NOTES

BONUS VERSE
Do not fear, for I am with you; do not be afraid, for I am your God. I will strengthen you; I will help you; I will hold on to you with my righteous right hand.
Isaiah 41:10

Fear thou not; for I am with thee: be not dismayed; for I am thy God: I will strengthen thee; yea, I will help thee; yea, I will uphold thee with the right hand of my righteousness.
Isaiah 41:10 (KJV)

**LEADER PACK
ITEMS USED TODAY:**
ITEMS 1, 2, 4, and 10–13

START IT (7 MINUTES)

1. Say: "Welcome back to Twists & Turns! Today we're kicking things off with a game called 'Will It Float?'"

2. Form three or four teams and provide each team one of the items you gathered for the game. Explain that you know for a fact that each of these items will sink when it's placed in the water. Say that you will give kids two minutes to try to build a raft that will make their items float.

3. Provide chenille stems and small pieces of corkboard or pool noodle and time kids for two minutes as they work on their flotation devices.

4. Guide kids to place their items in the water all at the same time and see which one floats (or floats the longest).

5. Congratulate the winning team and guide kids to find a spot to sit on the gameboard path you created for Day 1 "Start It."

6. Ask: "Was it hard or easy to make your team's item float?" Say: "In today's story, we're going to learn about something incredible that happened. Jesus didn't just float on top of the water; He walked on top of the water. When that happened, Peter learned a big lesson. He learned that Jesus is trustworthy even when we doubt!"

7. Ask a volunteer to add the Day 2 "Twists & Turns Banner Add-on" (item 2) to the "Twists & Turns Banner" (item 1). Ask a volunteer to read the caption aloud.

LEARN IT (12 MINUTES)

1. Say: "Yesterday we saw Jesus do something only God can do. Does anyone remember what He did?" *(He caused Peter and the other fishermen to catch so many fish that their nets couldn't hold them all.)*

2. Explain that the Bible has many stores about things Jesus did that show He is God. Provide each child with a small stone.

3. Say: "Remember, all of these stories that we're reading about Jesus and Peter are true. They really happened! In today's story, from the book of Matthew, Peter finds himself in a pretty crazy situation! I want you to listen for the moment when Peter starts to doubt that Jesus can take care of him. When you hear it, drop your stone into the water."

4. Display the "Day 2 Bible Story Picture" (pack item 10).

5. Open your Bible to Matthew 14. Tell the Bible story below, or use your own words.

PETER WALKED TO JESUS ON THE WATER

People followed Jesus everywhere He went. They wanted to hear Him teach about God. After a long day of teaching near the Sea of Galilee, Jesus said goodbye to the crowds and told His disciples to go ahead of Him in a boat. Then Jesus went up on a mountain to pray.

Late at night, the disciples' boat was far from shore. The wind began to blow and the water grew rough and choppy. The waves beat against their boat while the winds pushed harder and harder against them.

Very early in the morning, the disciples saw something coming toward them. It was Jesus walking on top of the water as if it were solid ground. The disciples cried out in fear, "It's a ghost!"

START IT PREP
- ❑ Pack items 1 and 2
- ❑ Timer
- ❑ Water
- ❑ Plastic storage tub
- ❑ Small pieces of corkboard or pool noodle
- ❑ 3–4 items of different sizes, weights, and shapes that will sink in water
- ❑ Chenille stems
- ❑ Paper towels
- ❑ Gameboard path from Day 1 "Start It"
  - Fill the tub halfway with water.
  - Display the "Twists & Turns Banner" (item 1) on a focal wall. Place the Day 2 "Twists and Turns Banner Add-on" (item 2) nearby.

LEADER TIP
- ❑ If you are short on time, just test items to see if they sink or float. Omit the flotation devices.

LEARN IT PREP
- ❑ Pack item 10
- ❑ Plastic storage tub filled with water from "Start It"
- ❑ Small stones or other simple objects that will sink—select objects that will fit in kids' memory maker bags
- ❑ Small basket
- ❑ Paper towels
  - Display the "Day 2 Bible Story Picture" (item 10) on a focal wall or place near your Bible to hold up as you tell the story.

But Jesus called out to them, "Don't be afraid! I am Jesus!"

Peter said, "If it is really You, Jesus, tell me to walk on top of the water to You."

So Jesus said, "Come."

Peter climbed out of the boat and began walking on the water toward Jesus. How amazing! But then Peter began to notice how strong the wind was and got scared. He began to sink into the dark, stormy water. Peter cried out, "Lord, save me!"

Immediately, Jesus reached out, grabbed Peter, and pulled him back up on top of the water. Jesus asked Peter, "Why did you doubt Me? Is your faith really so small?"

As soon as Jesus and Peter got back into the boat, the wind stopped! Everything was calm. Not only could Jesus walk on water, He could also control the wind and the waves! The disciples worshiped Jesus and said, "It's true. You really are the Son of God!"

Matthew 14:22-33

6. Talk through some of the following points with kids. For additional review and discussion questions refer to the back of the "Day 2 Bible Story Picture" (item 10).

    - What did the disciples see while they were out on the boat? *(Jesus walking toward them on the water)*
    - What was the first thing Jesus said to the disciples when they saw Him? *("Don't be afraid.")* Why do you think Jesus said that? *(They thought He was a ghost. He was in control of the situation. He knew everything would be okay.)*
    - Peter did something pretty brave. What did he do? *(He asked Jesus to let him walk on the water.)*
    - When did Peter start to doubt that Jesus could take care of him? *(when he saw how strong the wind was)*
    - Point out what happened when kids dropped their rocks in the water. They sank! That's exactly what happened to Peter when he forgot that he could trust Jesus.
    - When Peter cried out to Jesus and asked for help, what did Jesus do right away? *(He reached out and grabbed Peter, saving him from sinking.)*
    - After Jesus and Peter got back in the boat, the wind stopped. Jesus showed that He has control over everything, and we can trust Him!

KNOW IT (4 MINUTES)

1. Read the theme verse aloud from the "Theme Verse Poster" (item 4) and say: "One way we can know which paths God has for us is to study our Bibles. We can learn about who Jesus is and why we should trust Him, just like we did in today's story."

2. Give the kids the water mats you prepared and challenge them to manipulate the foam pieces inside to put the Bible verse in order.

3. For an extra challenge, cover the poster and encourage the kids to arrange the verse from memory.

LIVE IT (5 MINUTES)

1. Give the kids their activity books and some crayons. Guide them to turn to page 4.

2. Choose a volunteer to quickly recap today's Bible story.

3. Give the kids Bibles and guide them to focus on page 5 of their activity books.

4. Say: "One thing we learned in today's Bible story is that Jesus is trustworthy. That means we can trust Him to help us during tough situations."

5. Explain that kids may choose any verse on the left side of the "screen" to find in their Bibles. Once kids have read their verses, ask them to use crayons to color the dots from the verse to a time when they need to remember that Jesus is trustworthy. *(There are no wrong answers!)* Guide kids to find more verses as time allows.

6. ✝ Jesus proves He is trustworthy, and that is why we know we can trust Him as our Savior. Every person sins and disobeys God. But Jesus came to offer forgiveness for our sin. We can trust that His forgiveness is real, and we can choose to receive that gift.

7. Say: "Receiving God's gift of forgiveness and choosing to follow Jesus is one of the most important decisions a person can ever make! We'll keep learning about how to do that during VBS."

8. Offer to answer any questions kids may have before moving to the next activity.

FINISH IT (2 MINUTES)

1. Give the kids Day 2 tags to add to their Memory Maker bags. Discuss the wave icon and the words "Jesus Is Trustworthy" on the tag. Connect these back to the Bible story.

2. Provide small rocks from "Learn It" to add to Memory Maker bags as well. Gather the bags to save until tomorrow.

3. Challenge the kids to think of one person they could tell today's Bible story to.

4. Pray for kids to see and understand that Jesus is trustworthy.

LEADER TIP
Ask a helper to remove the rocks from the water, dry them off with paper towels and set them aside for later in the session.

KNOW IT PREP
- ❑ Pack item 4
- ❑ Gallon-size ziplock bags
- ❑ Water
- ❑ Blue food color
- ❑ Foam sheets
- ❑ Scissors
- ❑ Duct tape
- ❑ Permanent marker
  - Cut the foam sheets into short strips and write a word or phrase of Psalm 25:4 on each one with a permanent marker. Place the strips inside a bag and fill ⅓ full of water. Add a few drops of blue food coloring. Carefully press to remove as much air as possible and seal the bag. Double bag to prevent leaks, then use the duct tape to secure all four sides. Make one bag for each child or for pairs or teams of kids.
  - Display the "Theme Verse Poster" (item 4)

SHARING THE GOSPEL
The ✝ identifies an opportune time to share the gospel as led by the Holy Spirit.

LIVE IT PREP
- ❑ *VBS 2023 Kids Activity Books*
- ❑ Bibles (1 per kid)
- ❑ Crayons

FINISH IT PREP
- ❑ *VBS 2023 Memory Maker* and Day 2 tags
- ❑ Rocks from "Learn It"
- ❑ Basket to hold Memory Makers each day (optional)

WHEN CAN I TRUST JESUS?

(Application Activity #1—10 minutes)

- ❑ Pack item 11
- ❑ Bibles
- ❑ Markers or crayons
- ❑ Paper clips
- ❑ Brads
- ❑ Cardstock
- Mark Psalm 62:8; John 14:27; Psalm 91:1; Psalm 121:1-2; Psalm 9:10; 2 Timothy 1:7; John 16:33; and Psalm 27:1 in Bibles (1 or 2 references per Bible).
- Copy "When Can I Trust Jesus?" (item 11) onto cardstock so each kid will have a spinner circle. Cut circles apart.

1. Say: "Sometimes things happen in life that make us nervous or afraid, just like the storm scared Peter."
2. Tell the kids a simple example of a time you were afraid or worried.
3. Remind kids that, just like Peter, they can ask Jesus for help when they are afraid. They can also find verses in the Bible that can comfort and encourage them.
4. Allow volunteers to read aloud the verses you've marked.
5. Give each of the kids a copy of "When Can I Trust Jesus?" (item 11), and a marker or some crayons and point out that the verses you read are on the spinners.
6. Say: "In each of these spaces, write a time in your life when you should trust Jesus. We can trust Jesus with big and little things in our lives."
7. Guide the kids to color and decorate their spinners with crayons. Provide paper clips and brads and help kids attach the paper clips to the centers of their spinners. Attach brads loosely so the paper clips will spin.
8. Allow kids to take turns spinning each others' spinners, learning from each other about times when they can trust Jesus and what the Bible says that may help in that situation.

GET OUT OF THE BOAT

(Application Activity #2—10 minutes)

- ❑ Dry erase board and markers (optional)
- Clear a large area to play this active game.
- Familiarize yourself with the phrases and corresponding actions below. Consider writing the phrases and actions on a dry erase board for visual learners.

1. Say: "We're going to play a game called 'Get Out of the Boat!' Shout it out if you know who got out of the boat in today's story!" *(Peter)*
2. Explain that you will say four different phrases in a random order. The kids' job is to do the action for each phrase as quickly as possible.
3. Practice the phrases and corresponding actions below with the kids a few times before you start playing. Then, play!
4. **Leader Tip:** If you have a competitive group, eliminate the last person who does the action each time until you're down to a final player.

THE PHRASES:

- "Look, it's Jesus!"
  ➜ Run backward toward the back wall.
- "Get out of the boat!"
  ➜ Take giant steps toward the leader.
- "Help, I'm sinking!"
  ➜ Crawl toward the front wall.
- "Ride the waves!"
  ➜ Sit down where you are and rock back and forth.

5. Play several rounds. Then ask the kids how Peter probably felt at the beginning, the middle, and the end of today's story.

ON A ROLL

(Bible Skills Activity—10 minutes)

- ❑ Pack item 12
- ❑ Bibles
- ❑ *VBS 2023 Giant Inflatable Game Cubes* (2) (9781087779812) or 2 square cardboard boxes (square tissue boxes work well, as do larger options)
- ❑ Paper
- ❑ Markers
- ❑ Tape

- Display the "Books of the Bible Poster" (item 12) on a focal wall.
- Write Bible skills and actions on pieces of paper. Slide paper into the pockets of the game cubes or tape to each side of the boxes.
  - Cube 1: *Find an Old Testament book; Find a New Testament book; Find a book that begins with the letter J; Find one of the four gospels; Find the second chapter of any book; Find the book of Psalms.*
  - Cube 2: *Hop on one foot; Spin in circles; Run in place; Skip around the room; Leap across the room; Balance a book on your head.*

1. Allow the kids to take turns rolling the game cubes. They will follow the instructions on the cubes by combining the two actions they roll. (For instance, find an Old Testament book in the Bible while hopping on one foot.)

2. You can make this game competitive by forming two teams and guiding a player from each team to race to complete the actions first.

3. Encourage the kids to use the "Books of the Bible Poster" (item 12) and the Table of Contents in their Bibles for help.

Item 12

TIC-TAC-VERSE-KNOW

(Bonus Verse Activity—10 minutes)

- ❑ Pack item 13
- ❑ Dry erase board, marker, and eraser
- Display the "Day 2 Bonus Verse Poster: Isaiah 41:10" (item 13).
- Draw a tic-tac-toe board on the dry erase board. Write words or phrases of the verse across the squares in order.

1. Read the "Day 2 Bonus Verse Poster: Isaiah 41:10" (item 13) together.

2. Ask: "Are you ever afraid of things? Peter was afraid in today's story, wasn't he? What was Peter afraid of?" *(the strong wind when he was walking on the water)*

3. Say: "God tells us again and again that if we trust in Him, He will never leave us. We don't have to be afraid when we know Jesus. We can trust Him!"

4. Group the kids into two teams and assign one team *X*s and one team *O*s. Explain that they are going to play tic-tac-toe, but before they can play, they'll have to erase the word or phrase in the square where they want to go. Then, before marking their *X* or *O*, they have to say the verse, including the missing words or phrases.

5. Play the game. The first team to get three *X*s or *O*s in a row wins.

6. If the game is tied, a kid can win the game for his team by saying the verse with his back to the verse poster and the gameboard.

DO NOT FEAR, FOR	I AM WITH YOU;	DO NOT BE AFRAID,
FOR I AM YOUR GOD.	I WILL STRENGTHEN YOU;	I WILL HELP YOU;
I WILL HOLD ON TO YOU	WITH MY RIGHTEOUS	RIGHT HAND. ISAIAH 41:10

DAY 3: JESUS IS FORGIVING

BIBLE STORY

Peter Denied Jesus and Was Restored
(Luke 22:31-34,54-62; John 18:15-18; John 21:1-19)

TODAY'S POINT

Jesus is forgiving even when I sin.

BIBLE VERSE

Make your ways known to me, LORD; teach me your paths. *Psalm 25:4*

Shew me thy ways, O LORD; teach me thy paths. *Psalm 25:4* (KJV)

LEADER DEVOTION

God knows everything that is happening all the time. We know that. However, during the excruciating hours between Jesus' arrest and final breath on the cross, my mind wants to think everything else stopped. However, even as Jesus was stepping in to be our Redeemer, He was fully aware of the falling away of Peter. Even then, Jesus had plans to redeem and restore this soon-to-be church leader.

Jesus prayed for Peter and told Peter so. Peter declared that he would follow Jesus to prison or even to death. Jesus said Peter would deny he knew Jesus that very night before the rooster crowed.

As Jesus stood before the high priest, Peter tentatively followed and stood near a fire in the high priest's courtyard. Three times Peter was asked if he was one of the men who traveled with Jesus. Each time Peter's "no" was issued with increasing vehemence. The rooster crowed. Peter looked up and met Jesus' eyes. Peter left, weeping bitterly.

Based on Scripture, it appears Peter was not around as Jesus was led away to be crucified or when Jesus breathed His last breath. He didn't follow to see where Joseph and Nicodemus placed Jesus' body, though he raced to the tomb when Mary told the disciples that Jesus' body was missing.

Peter was one of the people to whom Jesus appeared the day of His resurrection. Twice more, Peter was in a locked room with the disciples when Jesus appeared. Still the memory of his emphatic, "No, I don't know Him!" must have rung in his ears.

Sometime later, Peter and six of the other disciples decided to go fishing. They fished all night but caught nothing. Early the next morning, a man on the shore called out the question most fishermen who have caught nothing hate to hear, "Got any fish?" Then the man said, "Toss your net on the right side of the boat." Suddenly the net was so full that seven grown men, many of whom had experience with this type of fishing, could not pull the net in. That's when John recognized the man. It was Jesus!

All the disciples in the boat shared this experience, but let's focus on things that may have been impactful for Peter. First, the miraculous catch of fish had to create immediate flashbacks to the first catch of fish when Jesus called Peter to be His disciple. Peter may have remembered his overwhelming sense of unworthiness and Jesus' promise that Peter would become a fisher of men.

Then, this same Peter who boldly stepped out on stormy seas to walk to Jesus but sank due to fear now plunged into the water in his rush to get to Jesus on the shore.

John's gospel explains that when the disciples got to shore, they saw a charcoal fire there with bread and fish. Interestingly, when John described the fire in the high priest's courtyard the night Jesus was arrested, he called it a "charcoal fire." (John 18:18) Sights and smells are often memory triggers. Could the sight of the charcoal fire and the smell of the smoke have triggered guilt in Peter as he remembered the moments when he denied knowing Jesus?

Possibly the most significant parallel happened after breakfast when Jesus spoke directly to Peter. Peter had denied Jesus three times. Now Jesus asked Peter three times, "Do you love Me?" Peter affirmed his love for Jesus all three times. The grief Peter felt may have been evidence of Peter's repentant heart. After each affirmation, Jesus gave Peter the command to take care of "My" sheep. Jesus recommissioned Peter as group leader and under shepherd.

Jesus is just as interested in the details of the lives of the kids you teach. What a privilege to have this opportunity to help kids know Jesus wants a personal relationship with each of them, and He has unique plans for each of their lives.

REFLECT

- Even when you're failing, Jesus has already written the story of your restoration. What things hover in your thoughts that make you feel unworthy of Jesus?
- What moments cause you to rush to Jesus?
- If Jesus looked you in the eye and said, "Do you love Me?" what would be your honest answer?

NOTES

BONUS VERSE
In him we have redemption, the forgiveness of sins.
Colossians 1:14

In whom we have redemption through his blood, even the forgiveness of sins.
Colossians 1:14 (KJV)

LEADER PACK ITEMS USED TODAY:
ITEMS 1, 2, 4, 12, and 14–19

START IT PREP

❏ Pack items 1 and 2
❏ Rubber chicken
❏ Resistance band (or similar stretchy item)
❏ Plastic cups
❏ Painter's tape
❏ Table
  • Set up the plastic cups on a table in a pyramid shape. Make a tape line on the floor about 8–10 feet away so the teams know how far back they need to stand to play.
  • Display the "Twists and Turns Banner" (item 1) on a focal wall and place the Day 3 "Twists and Turns Banner Add-on" (item 2) nearby.

SHARING THE GOSPEL

The ✝ identifies an opportune time to share the gospel as led by the Holy Spirit.

LEARN IT PREP

❏ Pack items 14 and 15
❏ Bible
❏ Small ziplock bag
❏ Fish-shaped crackers
❏ Glass jar with a lid
❏ Vegetable oil
❏ Water
❏ Blue food color
❏ Marker
  • Draw criss-crossed diagonal lines on the ziplock bag with a marker to indicate a fisherman's net. Place the fish-shaped crackers inside.
  • Color water with blue food color and fill the jar half full of water. Fill the remainder with vegetable oil and put the lid on the jar. The two won't mix, creating the appearance of waves of water.
  • Display the "Day 3 Bible Story Picture" (item 14) on a focal wall or place near your Bible to hold up as you tell the story.
  • Copy and cut apart a set of "Face the Feelings" cards (item 15) for each kid.

START IT (5 MINUTES)

1. Welcome kids as they arrive in the Bible Study Game Room. Group kids into two teams. Display a rubber chicken.

2. Say: "Welcome back to VBS! We're kicking off our time together with a game called Chicken Chunking!"

3. Explain that their teams are going to take turns using a resistance band to catapult the chicken toward a stack of cups. The team that manages to knock down the most cups wins.

4. Allow the kids to take a few practice turns. Then play the game.

5. Say: "One interesting fact about today's Bible story is: there's a chicken in it. A rooster, in fact. And it actually plays an important part in the story, because God used a rooster to remind Peter that he was a sinner."

6. ✝ Explain that *sin* is anything we think, say, or do that breaks God's law. Sin is disobedience against God, and the Bible tells us that every single person who ever lived was and is a sinner, except for one.

7. Remind the kids that on Day 1 you talked about how Jesus is holy. Jesus is the only perfect person who ever lived.

8. Say: "Because Jesus is perfect and we are sinners, sin keeps us separated from Him. But thankfully, He is willing to forgive us when we sin if we will receive His gift of forgiveness. We're going to learn more about that in today's Bible story."

9. Ask a volunteer to add the Day 3 "Twists & Turns Banner Add-on" (item 2) to the banner (item 1). Guide a volunteer to read the caption aloud.

LEARN IT (12 MINUTES)

1. Display the "Day 3 Bible Story Picture" (item 14).

2. Say: "Let's think about what we have seen happening with Peter and Jesus in the past two days."

3. Show the kids the bag of fish-shaped crackers. Ask: "What do these fish remind you of? What happened in our Day 1 story?" Allow volunteers to briefly recall the story.

4. Show them the jar of oil and water. Ask: "What happened on the water in yesterday's story?" *(Jesus and Peter walked on it.)*

5. Remind the kids that in both of these true stories we saw Jesus proving He is God through the things He did that only God can do.

6. Say: "Today we're learning from the Bible about some sad things that happened. Peter sinned, and Jesus died. But wonderful things happened, too! Jesus rose from the grave! That's right, He didn't stay dead. Just like He told His disciples, He came to life again after three days. Jesus showed Peter and all of us that we can be forgiven for our sins."

7. Give each kid a set of "Face the Feelings" cards (item 15). Explain that as kids listen to the story, you will pause to ask how they think Peter may have been feeling. They will choose the corresponding emotion card to show you.

8. Open your Bible to Luke 22. Tell the Bible story in your own words, using the next page as a guide. Stop when you see a smiley face and ask the kids how they think Peter must have been feeling at that point in the story.

PETER DENIED JESUS AND WAS RESTORED

Jesus knew He would soon be arrested, crucified, and buried in a tomb. And, He knew He would be resurrected on the third day. Jesus even knew His disciples would be afraid and abandon Him for a while. Jesus told Peter that difficult times were coming and Jesus had prayed for Peter. Peter declared that he would follow Jesus to prison or even to death. Jesus replied that Peter would deny he knew Jesus three times that very night before the rooster crowed. ☺

Later that night, in the garden of Gethsemane, soldiers came and arrested Jesus. ☺ They took Him to the high priest's house and made up charges against Jesus. Peter followed at a distance. Several people were sitting around a charcoal fire. Peter joined them. A woman in the group recognized Peter and said, "This man was with Him." Peter declared, "I don't know Him." Then someone else saw Peter, "You are one of them too." Peter again declared, "I am not!" ☺ About an hour later another person said, "I am certain this man was with Him." Peter replied, "I don't know what you are talking about!" Just then a rooster crowed. Jesus turned and looked right at Peter. Peter remembered what Jesus had said. ☺ Peter left, filled with shame and crying with regret.

The next day, Jesus was crucified and died on a cross. His body was buried in a tomb. On the third day, Jesus rose from the dead! Jesus then appeared to Peter and the rest of the disciples that day and again a week later. ☺

Some time later Peter decided to go fishing. Six of the other disciples went with him. They fished all night but caught nothing. The next morning a man on the shore called out, "Friends, you don't have any fish, do you?" The disciples answered no. The man said, "Cast the net on the right side of the boat." They did and the net filled with so many fish they could not haul it in. Suddenly John, one of the disciples, realized the man was Jesus! He told Peter, "It is the Lord!" ☺

Peter plunged into the water and swam to shore. Jesus had a charcoal fire ready and asked them to bring some of the fish. There were 153 fish in the net! Jesus took the bread and fish that He had cooked and shared it with them. After they had eaten, Jesus asked Peter, "Do you love Me?" Peter replied, "Yes, Lord, You know I love You." Jesus asked a second and a third time. Each time Peter answered yes. Each time Jesus told Peter to take care of His sheep (that meant the other followers of Jesus). Peter had denied Jesus, but Jesus knew Peter was ready to return to following Him. ☺

Luke 22:31-34,54-62; John 18:15-18; 21:1-19

LEADER TIP:
Kids may suggest a variety of different emotions at a given moment. Allow kids with different opinions to explain their choices. For example: when Jesus said Peter would deny Him, Peter may have been angry or sad that Jesus said this, or else afraid that it might be true (or all three at the same time).

9. Ask: "Why do you think Peter told people that he didn't know who Jesus was? How was Peter feeling the night Jesus was arrested and accused of doing things He didn't do?" *(He was scared.)*

10. Say: "Why do you think Peter was so sad that what Jesus said really happened?" *(Peter wanted to be loyal to Jesus, and, instead, Peter said he didn't know Jesus.)*

11. Explain that while there are a lot of sad things about today's story, like Peter's denials and Jesus' death, Jesus did rise from the dead in three days, just like He said He would! This is very good news. It means that Jesus died to take the punishment for our sin and that He has power over death because He is God the Son.

SHARING THE GOSPEL

The identifies an opportune time to share the gospel as led by the Holy Spirit.

KNOW IT PREP
☐ Pack items 4 and 14
☐ Allergy Alert
☐ Tape
☐ Permanent marker
☐ Balloons
☐ Straight pin
☐ Feathers (optional)
- Blow up balloons and write a word from the theme verse on each balloon. Tape the balloons to the wall in order within reach of kids. (For added connection to the rooster in today's story, place a feather inside each balloon.)
- Display the "Theme Verse Poster" (item 4) on the focal wall. Place the "Day 3 Bible Story Picture" (item 14) facedown, within easy reach.

LEADER TIP
Post an allergy alert if using latex balloons. Carefully clean up any scraps of balloon as they can be a choking hazard.

LIVE IT PREP
☐ VBS 2023 Kids Activity Books
☐ Pencils

FINISH IT PREP
☐ VBS 2023 Kids Memory Maker and Day 3 tags
☐ Feathers from "Know It" if used
☐ Basket to hold Memory Makers each day (optional)

---

12. 🔾 Say, "Jesus showed He had forgiven Peter by telling Peter about His plans for Peter's life. He wanted Peter to tell others the good news about Jesus' forgiveness and to take care of and teach the people who followed Jesus. That's exactly what Peter ended up doing. He spent the rest of his life teaching others about who Jesus is. Jesus showed Peter and you and me that we can be forgiven when we sin. Emphasize that in order to receive His forgiveness, we must confess our sins to Jesus and ask Him to forgive us."

KNOW IT (5 MINUTES)

1. Review the "Theme Verse Poster" (item 4). Cover or remove the verse from view.
2. Use "Review Questions" on the back of the "Day 3 Bible Story Picture" (item 14) to review the story. Each time a child answers a question correctly, give her the opportunity to pop one of the balloons with a straight pin. Then she will lead the group in saying the verse, including the missing word. Carefully collect the straight pin between uses.
3. Continue until all of the balloons have been popped and the group is saying the verse with no balloons as hints.

LIVE IT (5 MINUTES)

1. Give the kids their activity books and pencils and lead them to turn to page 6. Ask a volunteer to name the thing that Peter did in today's story that he regretted. *(He denied that he knew Jesus.)*
2. Ask the kids to look at page 7. Explain that they are going to place their pencils on the golf balls and close their eyes, trying to draw a line to the hole without looking. If their lines cross any hazards, they need to use their Bibles to find the verses.
3. 🔾 Say: "The Bible says we all sin, just like Peter did when he denied Jesus. But there is forgiveness for all of us if we confess our sins to Jesus and ask Him to forgive us."
4. Challenge the kids to unscramble the word under "Level Up!" *(confess)*

FINISH IT (3 MINUTES)

1. Give the kids Day 3 tags to add to their Memory Maker bags. Ask kids what the heart icon has to do with the words "Jesus is forgiving" and today's Bible story. Provide one feather from "Know It" (if used) to each kid and ask how these relate to today's story. Guide kids to add these to their Memory Makers as well.
2. Gather the Memory Makers to save until tomorrow.
3. Challenge the kids to tell their families about today's story.
4. Ask a volunteer to pray that today would continue to be a day of learning about the forgiveness of Jesus.

A DAY IN THE LIFE

(Application Activity #1—10 minutes)

❑ Pack items 16, 17, and 18

❑ Dice—1 or 2 to move faster or slower

❑ Small stones or pennies (1 per kid)

❑ Bible

• Copy and cut apart enough "Twists & Turns Response Cards" (item 16) for each kid.

• Cut apart the "Gospel Stop Explanations" cards from item 17. Place each card at a corresponding verse in your Bible.

❑ Lay the "A Day in the Life Gameboard" (item 18) on the floor.

1. Give each kid a penny or small stone to use as a game piece. (Option: to help the game move faster, group the kids into teams of 3–4 and give each team a game piece.)

2. Say that you will play a game called "A Day in the Life." Explain the information on the instruction sheet (item 17) to kids.

3. Indicate the gospel icons on the gameboard.

4. Say: "If you land on a 'Gospel Stop' space, you must stop and wait while a card is read. If you land on a space with a number, you must go forward (+) or backward (-) that many spaces."

5. ✝ Use a "Gospel Stop Explanation" card to explain each gospel icon each time someone lands there.

6. Emphasize that unexpected things, good and bad, will happen, but the most important thing is that we have a relationship with Jesus. Trusting Jesus as Savior means He provides forgiveness for our sins and the promise of eternal life with Him.

7. Distribute "Twists & Turns Response Cards" and request that kids fill them out. Explain that there are no wrong answers, this is simply to help them, and you, understand where they may be along the path to salvation. Promise that you will be discreet with their answers and not share them with other kids. Make a plan to follow up with kids who indicate they have questions or are ready to make a decision.

QUICK DRAW

(Application Activity #2—10 minutes)

❑ Dry erase board, markers, and eraser

❑ Paper strips

❑ Pen

❑ Cup

❑ Timer (optional)

• Choose phrases to represent simple scenes from today's story and write them on strips of paper. Examples include: *Peter cried; Jesus rose again; Peter jumped out of the boat; Jesus cooked fish; Peter went fishing;* and *The nets were full of fish.* Place the strips of paper in a cup.

1. Group the kids into two teams.

2. Say: "We're going to see if we can remember some things that happened in today's Bible story. We're playing a game called 'Quick Draw.' One person on your team will choose a piece of paper that contains a phrase about something that happened in today's story. She'll have one minute to draw that part of the story for your team to guess. For instance, your paper might say, 'The rooster crowed.'"

3. Explain that the other team will remain silent while the drawing team is shouting out guesses. The team that guesses more drawings correctly wins. Use a timer if you need to limit the time kids have to guess to keep the game moving.

4. Guide kids to silently think of a time that they needed forgiveness like Peter did in today's story. Pray for kids, thanking God that He provides forgiveness through Jesus to people who receive it and follow Him.

Leader Note: The teams don't have to guess the phrase exactly as it's worded. They just need to identify the part of the story the drawing portrays.

READY TO ROLL

(Bible Skills Activity—10 minutes)

❏ Pack item 12

❏ Bibles (1 for every 2 kids)

❏ Dice (1 for every 2 kids)

• Display the "Books of the Bible Poster" (item 12).

1. Group kids into pairs and give each pair a Bible and a die.

2. Instruct the pairs to take turns rolling the die. When she rolls, the roller will say as many books of the Bible as the number she rolled. She may want to use the "Books of the Bible Poster" or the Table of Contents in the Bible if she needs help.

3. **Leader Note:** This activity is wonderful for kids who have little knowledge of the Bible. It helps to start familiarizing them with the books. If you have a more biblically literate group, challenge the kids to use their Bibles to find one book they name on each turn.

THE BIBLE VERSE EFFECT

(Bonus Verse Activity—10 minutes)

❏ Pack item 19

❏ Dominoes

❏ Permanent markers (2 colors)

❏ Masking tape

• Add tape to the back of each domino. Write one word from the verse on the back of each domino in the translation of your choice. Make two sets, one with each color of marker.

• Display the "Day 3 Bonus Verse Poster: Colossians 1:14" (item 19) on a focal wall.

1. Group the kids into two teams and give each team a set of Bible verse dominoes. Challenge the teams to set up the dominoes on their ends in Bible verse order, and then let kids knock dominoes down, creating a chain reaction.

2. In the second round, have the teams race to see who can set the verse up in order and knock it down first. If you have time for a third round, guide kids to flip dominoes to the number side and make a train of connecting numbers. Then guide kids to flip them over and quickly shuffle them into verse order.

3. Guide kids to say the verse together, removing one domino each time until they are saying the verse without reading.

DAY 4: JESUS IS WORTH FOLLOWING

BIBLE STORY

Peter Spoke Boldly about Jesus (Acts 3:1–4:24)

TODAY'S POINT

Jesus is worth following even when it gets tough.

BIBLE VERSE

Make your ways known to me, LORD; teach me your paths. *Psalm 25:4*

Shew me thy ways, O LORD; teach me thy paths. *Psalm 25:4* (KJV)

LEADER DEVOTION

What's your usual response when God doesn't seem to make sense? Maybe, like the man in today's story, your child was born with a disability you know will affect her for life. Maybe you are living with a health concern that has altered your life. Maybe your family has fallen on tough financial times. Maybe you're dealing with depression or anxiety or a broken relationship. Maybe, like Peter and John, you're facing persecution for your faith.

In this broken world, there's something you've asked God to change, and He hasn't seemed to act.

My theory is everyone has a go-to reaction in these situations. Some people jump straight to anger. Some resort to a curled-in-a-ball-can't-get-up-in-the-morning grief and sadness. Some people topple in anxiety: "Is God still in control?" Some people try to take over. "God won't do this for me? OK, I'll jump in and do it myself." Some people (ask me how I know) do all four and more.

We don't always leave room for this kind of talk. We're afraid we'll sound like "bad Christians," like we don't have enough faith. We hear that the early church members in Acts prayed for boldness and rejoiced to be persecuted. We think that means they didn't feel afraid or sad or angry. I think the fact that they had to pray for boldness means they didn't have anything close to boldness going into these situations. Just look at all the twists and turns Peter's faith journey has taken already this week in VBS. I think these early Christians were probably more like David.

"How long, LORD? Will you forget me forever? How long will you hide your face from me? How long will I store up anxious concerns within me, agony in my mind every day? How long will my enemy dominate me?" (Psalm 13:1-2)

God can handle these kinds of questions. The Bible shows us that. He doesn't turn away from hard moments. And, He proves again and again that He's worth following, even when it gets tough. That's why the man in our Acts 3 passage could immediately praise God when he was healed instead of crediting Peter and John with the miracle. That's why Peter and John could stand boldly before the Jewish leaders and speak the words God gave them.

Jesus is worth following because He has the power to heal.

Jesus is worth following because He gives us the words we need when we need them.

Jesus is worth following because He died to save us.

Even if Jesus had never done anything for us, He is still worth following because of who He is. A relationship with Him is a treasure greater than any silver or gold. Even when He doesn't seem to act, we can rest safely in that relationship like David did, knowing the truth of His character means that we can know that He is always working to make all things new.

"But I have trusted in your faithful love; my heart will rejoice in your deliverance. I will sing to the LORD because he has treated me generously." (Psalm 13:5-6)

REFLECT

- How has Jesus proven Himself worthy through His work in your life?
- Do you have any questions about tough situations in your life you've been avoiding asking Jesus? Make a list and take some time to walk through those with Jesus.
- Spend some time thanking Jesus for who He is and for the relationship you have with Him.

NOTES

BONUS VERSE

There is salvation in no one else, for there is no other name under heaven given to people by which we must be saved.
Acts 4:12

Neither is there salvation in any other: for there is none other name under heaven given among men, whereby we must be saved.
Acts 4:12 (KJV)

LEADER PACK ITEMS USED TODAY:
ITEMS 1, 2, 4, 12, and 20–23

START IT (3 MINUTES)

1. Guide kids to sit down, each on his own game space. Dim the lights in the room.

2. Ask: "Have you ever played hide-and-seek in the dark? It's easy to bump into stuff when it's dark, isn't it? One thing that helps is a flashlight!"

3. Show the kids the flashlight without batteries in it. Try turning it on. When it doesn't work, act like you're trying to figure out why. Then you realize there aren't any batteries inside. Put in the batteries and turn on the flashlight.

4. Say: "My flashlight needed power to work! In today's Bible story, we'll learn that Peter needed God's power to do some pretty difficult things he had to do."

5. Ask a volunteer to add the Day 4 "Twists & Turns Banner Add-on" (item 2) to the "Twists & Turns Banner" (item 1).

LEARN IT (12 MINUTES)

1. Keep the lights partially dimmed.

2. Display the "Bible Story Scenes" (item 20) and the "Day 4 Bible Story Picture" (item 21).

3. Distribute flashlights to kids.

4. Say: "Today's story takes place after Jesus rose from the dead and then returned to heaven. Remember when Jesus told Peter, 'Feed My sheep'? Well, in today's story we're going to see what Jesus meant by that. He knew that Peter would be a great teacher and someone who would tell many people about Jesus. He knew that Peter would continue to follow Him, even when it got hard."

5. Explain that in today's story we'll see that Peter needed God's power to help him be bold. Tell them that they are going to help you tell the story by shining their lights on some scenes from the story where Peter needed power from God.

6. Instruct them to turn their flashlights off and set them on the floor.

7. Open your Bible to Acts 3. Tell the Bible story in your own words. Use the Bible story text on the following page as a guide. When you come to the word "shine," guide kids to shine their lights on the Bible story picture that shows the scene.

START IT PREP
☐ Pack items 1 and 2
☐ Flashlight
☐ Batteries
☐ Gameboard path from Day 1 "Start It"
  • Remove any batteries that are currently in the flashlight.
  • Display the "Twists and Turns Banner" (item 1) on a focal wall and place the Day 4 "Twists & Turns Banner Add-on" (item 2) nearby.

LEARN IT PREP
☐ Pack items 20 and 21
☐ Small flashlights (1 per kid)
  • Cut apart the "Bible Story Scenes" (item 20) and display on a focal wall.
  • Display the "Bible Story Picture 4" (item 21) on a focal wall or place near your Bible to hold up as you tell the story.

LEADER TIP
Before you distribute flashlights, communicate clear expectations to kids: they will not shine the flashlights in anyone's eyes and will follow your instructions.

PETER SPOKE BOLDLY ABOUT JESUS

Peter and another disciple, John, were walking to the temple when they saw a man who couldn't walk, which meant he couldn't earn money to buy food. He begged Peter and John to give him money.

"I don't have silver or gold," Peter told the man, "but what I do have, I give you: in the name of Jesus, get up and walk!"

Through Jesus' power, the man was healed. **(Shine)** He was so excited. He entered the temple with them walking and leaping and praising God. The people in the temple knew the man and rushed over to ask what had happened.

Peter told the people that Jesus gave John and him the ability to heal the man. **(Shine)** He reminded the crowd about everything that had happened: how the crowd had handed Jesus over to the Roman authorities and asked for Him to be crucified. He said that just as the prophets predicted, Jesus suffered and died to take the punishment for our sins. Peter told them God had raised Jesus from the dead!

Peter asked the people to *repent*, which means to turn away from sin and to turn toward God, asking Him for forgiveness. He said God would forgive their sins.

The religious leaders heard what was happening and were angry that Peter and John were preaching about Jesus. They arrested Peter and John and put them in prison.

The next day, Peter and John stood before all the most important religious leaders. **(Shine)** The leaders asked them where they got the power to heal the man. Peter was filled with the Holy Spirit and spoke boldly. He told them the man was healed by Jesus' power. Peter told the leaders that trusting in Jesus and His power is the only way to be saved from the punishment for sin.

The leaders knew Peter and John did not have much education and were amazed at their confidence. They recognized that Peter and John could speak this way because they had been with Jesus. The leaders ordered Peter and John not to teach about Jesus and threatened them with worse punishments. Peter and John said, "We are unable to stop speaking about what we have seen and heard."

Peter and John knew it would be wrong to stop telling people about Jesus. They believed Jesus is worth following even when things get tough.

Acts 3:1–4:24

8. Use your flashlight to highlight each of the Bible story pictures. Allow kids to imitate you with their flashlights. Ask kids why Peter needed God's power in each situation.

9. Say: "Sometimes it's hard to follow Jesus. Life gets tough and we're faced with hard decisions. But it's worth it to love Him, to obey Him, and to live our lives for Him. He helps us in all kinds of ways, starting with saving us and forgiving us from our sins. After we choose to follow Him and have a relationship with Him, He is always with us, giving us strength to obey and to make it through hard situations. We can rely on His strength and power when we are going through tough things."

KNOW IT (6 MINUTES)

1. Group the kids into two teams and guide them to stand behind the "Start" line. About five or six feet from the line, lay out each team's set of Bible verse plates in random order.

2. Give each team three beanbags. Explain that one player from each team will try to toss a beanbag on the first word of the Bible verse. If he hits the first word before running out of beanbags, the player may collect that plate and move to the second word. After the first player runs out of beanbags, he will retrieve them and pass them to the next player. That player picks up where the first player left off.

3. Once a team has the first word, players will take turns tossing for the rest of the words in order. Each player may have three tries before passing his turn to the next player.

4. Each team should continue simultaneously until they have a full stack of Bible verse plates. Then they can work together to lay them out in verse order.

5. Allow kids to use the "Theme Verse Poster" (item 4) if needed.

6. If you have a competitive group, make this a race to see which team can get all of the plates and then put them in the correct order first.

7. Guide kids to toss beanbags on the three Bible story pictures (items 20 and 21) in the order they happened in the story, if time allows.

LIVE IT (6 MINUTES)

1. Give kids their activity books, Bibles, and pencils. Lead them to open to page 10.

2. Ask a volunteer to name one tough thing that Peter did in today's Bible story that required God's power to help him.

3. Lead the kids to look at page 11.

4. Say: "Finding these verses in your Bible will help you know which letters go in which blanks."

5. Help kids locate verses as needed. When the kids have filled in the blanks, read the statements together.

FINISH IT (3 MINUTES)

1. Give the kids Day 4 tags and paper flashlights to add to their Memory Maker bags. Review how the speech bubble *(Peter spoke to the people)* and the flashlight *(Jesus' power helps us during tough times, just like batteries power a flashlight)* relate to today's Bible story.

2. Challenge the kids to think of ways to tell someone in their home or friend group about Jesus' love, forgiveness, and power.

3. Pray for the kids, asking the Lord to help them understand the good news about Jesus.

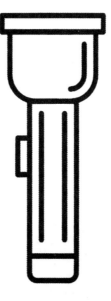

KNOW IT PREP
❑ Pack items 4, 20, and 21
❑ Paper plates
❑ Permanent marker
❑ Painter's tape
❑ 6 beanbags
  • Write the verse on paper plates, one word per plate. Make two full sets of the verse.
  • Use painter's tape to make a "Start" line for the teams to stand behind.
  • Display the "Theme Verse Poster" (item 4) on a focal wall. Place the "Bible Story Scenes" and "Day 4 Bible Story Picture" (items 20 and 21) nearby to use in the game.

LIVE IT PREP
❑ *VBS 2023 Kids Activity Books*
❑ Bibles
❑ Pencils

FINISH IT PREP
❑ *VBS 2023 Memory Maker* and Day 4 tags
❑ Yellow cardstock
  • Cut a flashlight shape from cardstock for each kid (trace the sketch if needed). Write *Jesus is worth following even when it gets tough* on each flashlight.
❑ Basket to hold Memory Makers each day (optional)

UPS AND DOWNS

(Application Activity #1—10 minutes)

- ❑ Pack item 22
- ❑ *VBS 2023 Memory Makers*
- ❑ Bibles (1 per group)
- ❑ Dice—(1 per group of 2–3 kids)
- ❑ Small stones
- • Copy the "Ups and Downs Gameboard" (item 22) for each kid.
- • Consider marking the following verses in each Bible to help kids who are new to the Bible locate the references more quickly: 2 Timothy 1:7; Deuteronomy 31:6; Hebrews 13:6; Joshua 1:9; Psalm 138:3; and Psalm 27:1.
1. Group the kids into pairs or groups of three. Give each group a Bible, an "Ups and Downs Gameboard" (item 22), a die, and small stones to use as game pieces.
2. Say: "In today's Bible story we saw that Peter was bold when he spoke to the religious leaders. He relied on God's strength. We're going to play a game and look up some Bible verses about being bold!"
3. Explain that each kid, on her turn, will roll a die to determine how many spaces she'll move. If she lands at the bottom of a rope, she will look up the verse in her Bible before climbing up the rope to the top. If she lands at the top of a fireman's pole, she has no choice but to slide all the way down to the bottom.
4. Play. Declare the first person from each group to reach the final space the winner.
5. As time allows, competitive groups can play tournament style until only one winner remains.
6. Give each kid an "Ups and Downs Gameboard" to take home.

CHITTER CHATTER

(Application Activity #2—10 minutes)

- ❑ Paper
- ❑ Marker
- ❑ Write the following phrases on pieces of paper:
  - • *Win eye mats cool*
  - • *Win sum won kneads add vice*
  - • *Win eye yam a frayed*
  - • *Win eyes pend tie mat hoe ma*
  - • *Win eye sea bads tough go win gone*
1. Say: "Peter was bold for Jesus. Jesus gave Peter courage to tell people the truth about who Jesus is. Now we're going to think about some times when you might need to be bold for Jesus."
2. Explain that kids will be reading a series of words that don't look like much of anything. The trick is to listen to the sounds to figure out the words.
3. Call on a volunteer to choose a piece of paper and read it aloud to the group, trying to get them to guess what it really means. After each phrase, discuss ways kids might need to be bold for Jesus in that particular situation.

KEY:
- • When I'm at school
- • When someone needs advice
- • When I am afraid
- • When I spend time at home
- • When I see bad stuff going on

THE LAST SHALL BE FIRST

(Bible Skills Activity—10 minutes)

- ❑ Pack item 12
- ❑ Bibles
- ❑ Index cards
- ❑ Markers
- • Display the "Books of the Bible Poster" (item 12) on a focal wall.
- • Write books of the Bible on index cards (1 book per card). Make enough cards for each team of 3 to have a set of 21 assorted books (with no duplicates).
- • **Leader Tip:** Consider using the book cards from several sets of the *KidMin Toolbox: Books of the Bible Flash Cards* (9781087772639) found on Lifeway.com instead of making your own.

1. Display the "Books of the Bible Poster" (item 12).
2. Lead kids to form groups of three. Give each group a Bible and a set of Bible book cards.
3. Explain that they will be playing a game where being last wins (sort of). One player will deal the cards facedown. Each player will keep his pile of cards facedown in front of him.
4. Instruct all three players to turn their top cards over at the same time. The person whose card is nearest the end of the Bible wins all three cards.
5. Encourage the kids to use the "Books of the Bible Poster" (item 12) or their Bibles to help them determine who wins each round.
6. The last player with cards is the winner!

JUST GUESS

(Bonus Verse Activity—10 minutes)

- ❑ Pack item 23
- ❑ Chairs (1 per kid)
- • Arrange chairs in a circle.
- • Display the "Day 4 Bonus Verse Poster: Acts 4:12" (pack item 23) on a focal wall.

1. Read Acts 4:12 together using the poster.
2. ✝ Say: "Jesus is the only One who can forgive us of our sins. There's no other way to be forgiven or to get to heaven. We have to know Him and have a relationship with Him in order to be saved. That's good news, though, because having a relationship with Jesus is really great!"
3. Ask kids to remind you what Jesus gave Peter the ability to do during today's Bible story *(heal the man, speak to the people, speak to the religious leaders).* Explain that Peter could only do these things because he had a relationship with Jesus!
4. Lead the kids to sit in chairs.
5. Say: "To have a relationship with people, you have to know them pretty well! We are going to learn more about each other in this game."
6. Explain that you will give "Guess who ..." clues. For instance, "Guess who has a dog." Then everyone who has a dog will stand, say the Bible verse together, and switch seats.
7. Warn kids that if you say, "Guess who is the only way to be saved from sin." then everyone will shout, "Jesus!" while switching seats.

POSSIBLE "GUESS WHO?" CLUES:
- Guess who plays a sport (or mention specifics: basketball, soccer, baseball, softball, football).
- Guess who likes video games.
- Guess who likes to draw.
- Guess who has a sister (or brother).
- Guess who has a cat.
- Guess who likes pizza.
- Guess who is allergic to chocolate.
- Guess who likes to go on trips.
- Guess who likes to read.
- Guess who went to VBS this summer.
- Guess who Jesus loves.
- Guess who likes board games.
- Guess who likes to play outside.

DAY 5: JESUS IS FOR EVERYONE

BIBLE STORY

Peter Told Cornelius about Jesus (Acts 10)

TODAY'S POINT

Jesus is for everyone, including me.

BIBLE VERSE

Make your ways known to me, LORD; teach me your paths. *Psalm 25:4*

Shew me thy ways, O LORD; teach me thy paths. *Psalm 25:4* (KJV)

LEADER DEVOTION

As we've followed Peter's journey with Jesus this week, we have seen him move from fishing for fish to fishing for people. His life changed when he recognized the holiness of Jesus. He had faith to walk on water—at least for a little while—and even though he feared for his life in the midst of unimaginable trials, twists, and turns, he loved Jesus deeply. Peter took Jesus' challenge to "feed my sheep" (John 21:17) very seriously. On Day 5 we get to walk beside Peter while he not only learned that Jesus is for everyone but also while he confidently shared what he had learned.

Until recently I had always skipped over the fact that Simon, who Peter was staying with at the time of today's story, was a tanner. It just seemed like a normal thing to say about someone when you're introducing him, "Hey, this is Simon. He's a leather-maker." However, this introduction would certainly translate differently to a Jewish person in the 1st century than it did to me—a Gentile in the 21st century. Being a tanner, working with animal hides, was an unclean profession. So then why was Peter even staying at Simon's house? Could God have been working in Peter's heart to help him understand "What God has made clean, do not call impure?" (Acts 10:15)

After all, God had already been working on Cornelius' heart. He was already interested in God and did a lot of "good" things. God heard his prayers and made a lot of things happen to make sure Cornelius and his family clearly heard the message of salvation.

- Cornelius had to recognize his vision was from God.
- He had to obey the message and send men to Joppa.
- The men had to go and find Peter.
- Peter had to go up to the roof to pray.
- God had to give Peter a vision for him to understand why he should go with the men.
- Peter had to understand and believe the vision.
- Peter had to go with the men to Caesarea when it was forbidden by the Jewish custom to associate with foreigners.
- Cornelius had to gather his friends and family.
- The friends and family had to accept the invitation and listen to Peter's message.
- Peter had to be bold and share a message that went against popular Jewish belief. At this point, many Jews believed that salvation was only for them. (See Romans 3:29.)
- Everyone gathered had to listen, allow their hearts to be open, and make decisions to place their faith in Jesus alone for salvation.

In God's perfect goodness, He arranged for all these things to happen so Cornelius could do more than just pray to God and give to charity. He did these things so he could understand how to have a personal relationship with God. If God made so many things happen for Cornelius to have a personal relationship with Him, God can do the same for you. He can do the same for your family, for your kids at VBS, and even for the people society wants to tell us aren't good enough. Jesus is for everyone.

Can you imagine what a privilege it must have been to share, for the very first time, that freedom from sin and the gift of eternal salvation are freely available to ALL people? Believers in Jesus still have the very same privilege that Peter had that day in Caesarea. For the person you share with today, it could be the very first time that he's ever heard the message of salvation too. What are you waiting for? Go tell someone!

REFLECT

- Take a few minutes to praise God for the miracle of your salvation. Write down some key things that took place for you to understand the gift of salvation.
- Thank God that the forgiveness of sins is available to anyone and everyone. Ask God to reveal at least one person you can share this amazing truth with this week.
- Think about the beautiful variety of kids you will lead at VBS. How can you best help them understand that no matter what their differences are, salvation in Jesus is for every single one of them?

NOTES

BONUS VERSE

All the prophets testify about him that through his name everyone who believes in him receives forgiveness of sins.
Acts 10:43

To him give all the prophets witness, that through his name whosoever believeth in him shall receive remission of sins.
Acts 10:43 (KJV)

LEADER PACK ITEMS USED TODAY:
ITEMS 1–4, 10, 12, 14, 21, 24–29

START IT PREP

☐ Pack items 1 and 2
☐ *VBS 2023 Music for Kids*
☐ 3 small balls with emoji faces
☐ Small bag
☐ Circle stickers
☐ Permanent marker
  • Use a permanent marker to mark one ball with an *L*, one with an *R*, and one with a *C*.
  • Place the balls in the bag.
  • Display the "Twists and Turns Banner" (item 1) on a focal wall and place the Day 5 "Twists and Turns Banner Add-on" (item 2) nearby.

TEACHER'S TIP

You can purchase balls with emoji faces on them or make your own by drawing faces on small foam balls, along with the letters.

LEARN IT PREP

☐ Pack items 24 and 25
☐ Pencils
  • Copy and cut apart enough "Bible Story Bingo" cards (item 24) for each kid to have one.
  • Display the "Day 5 Bible Story Picture" (item 25) on a focal wall, or place near your Bible to hold up as you tell the story.

LEADER TIPS

• See the definition of *vision* on the opposite page if it is a new term for kids.
• If you sense that the "Bible Story Bingo" activity will be too distracting for your group, tell the Bible story first and then distribute bingo cards, retelling the story as a review.

START IT (4 MINUTES)

1. Guide the kids to sit in chairs that form a circle.

2. Say: "Welcome back! Today we're going to start with a game called Musical Emojis!"

3. Explain that kids will pass the bag around the circle while the music plays. When it stops, the person holding the bag will pull a ball from inside. If the ball is marked with an *L*, the person to the left is out. If the ball is marked with an *R*, the person to the right is out. And if it's marked *C*, the person holding the bag is out.

4. Play the theme song as kids begin to pass the bag. To keep everyone involved in the game, instead of making kids sit out, use circle stickers to mark who gets out. If the bag lands on a person who is out, let him choose who to hand the bag to. Continue playing until there's only one person left who isn't marked (or time runs out).

5. Say: "You know, sometimes we get left out, or at least we feel like we do. Sometimes it feels like people sort of forget about us. But Jesus is nothing like that. He doesn't leave anyone out. He's for everyone, even you and me!"

6. Ask a volunteer to add the Day 5 "Twists & Turns Banner Add-on" (item 2) to the "Twists & Turns Banner" (item 1). Guide a volunteer to read the caption aloud.

LEARN IT (12 MINUTES)

1. Display the "Day 5 Bible Story Picture" (item 25).

2. Say: "In today's Bible story, two different men had visions. One is a man named Cornelius and the other is Peter. These visions from God helped both Cornelius and Peter understand that God doesn't love just one certain kind of person. He loves all people."

3. Explain that Peter was a Jew, but Cornelius wasn't. That means Peter was from a long line of people who worshiped God. Some people thought Jews were the only ones Jesus came to save, but God made it clear that Jesus came for all sorts of people from all sorts of places, including you and me!

4. Give each kid a "Bible Story Bingo" card (item 24) and a pencil.

5. Say: "During the story, listen carefully to hear some of the words on your bingo card. If you hear a word from your card, mark it out. Once you get four in a row, quietly turn your card over and put your pencil down." (Kids may also wish to continue marking words after they get four in a row to help them listen.)

6. Open your Bible to Acts 10. Guide kids to mark their respective free spaces. Tell the Bible story using your own words with the Bible story on the next page as a guide.

Item 24

PETER TOLD CORNELIUS ABOUT JESUS

Cornelius was a Roman army officer who lived in Caesarea (sess uh REE uh). He and everyone in his house worshiped **God**. He always prayed to God, and he generously gave to people who needed help. One afternoon he saw an **angel** of God in a **vision**.

The angel told him, "God has heard your **prayers**, and He has seen how you help others." Then the angel told Cornelius to send men to the city of Joppa and find a man named **Peter**. The angel told Cornelius where Peter was staying. Cornelius did what the angel said.

The next day, while the men were getting close to the city, Peter went to pray on the roof of the house where he was staying. He was **hungry** and wanted something to eat, but while lunch was being prepared, he had a vision. Peter saw something that looked like a large sheet coming down from **heaven**. There were all kinds of **animals**, reptiles, and birds in the sheet. A voice said to him, "Get up, Peter; kill and eat."

These were animals that were forbidden by God's laws to be eaten, so Peter said, "No, Lord. I have never eaten anything that is unclean." The voice said to him again, "Do not call something unclean if God has made it clean." This happened three times.

Peter was confused. While he was trying to understand what the vision meant, the men looking for him arrived at the gate. The **Holy Spirit** told Peter, "Three men are here looking for you. Get up, go downstairs, and go with them because I have sent them." The men told Peter about Cornelius and about how an angel had told Cornelius to send for Peter.

The next day Peter went with the men to Caesarea. Cornelius had gathered his **family** and friends to hear Peter's message. Peter said, "You know it is against our laws for a Jewish person and a non-Jewish person to visit together in a home. But God has shown me not to think of people in this way."

Peter spoke, "God does not show favoritism. Every person can be seen as right or acceptable to God through faith in Him. Jesus is Lord of all." He reminded them that they knew **Jesus** had performed **miracles**. The people who had been with Jesus saw Him be put to death on a **cross**. But God raised Him to life on the third day. Jesus told His followers to tell more people about Him. Peter explained that everyone who believes in Jesus will have their sins forgiven.

While Peter was speaking, the Holy Spirit came down on everyone who heard the message, not just the Jews. Peter commanded them to be **baptized** in the name of Jesus, and they asked Peter to stay with them for a few days.

Acts 10

7. Congratulate the kids who found four in a row. Call on kids to name something they marked off, and then ask volunteers to share what they remember about how it fit into the story.

8. ✝ Say: "I'm so glad that Jesus included all kinds of people when He came to rescue us from our sin. He included you too, you know! If you want to learn more about how to become a follower of Christ, let's talk about it today!"

9. Allow a few minutes to answer any questions kids may ask in the group setting. Invite kids to talk to a leader if they'd prefer to talk one-on-one.

HELPFUL DEFINITIONS
Vision—one way God communicates with people; it is like experiencing a dream except the person is awake
Unclean—describes something that Jewish law said people could not use or do
Favoritism—treating one person or group of people as more special or important than another

SHARING THE GOSPEL
The ✝ identifies an opportune time to share the gospel as led by the Holy Spirit.

LEADER TIP
Talking about salvation with a child can be a private conversation, but do not be alone with a child. Always have another adult within eyesight. Whenever possible, involve parents in these important conversations as well!

KNOW IT PREP
❑ Pack item 4
❑ Timer
❑ Dry erase board and markers or poster board and permanent markers (3 colors of marker)
  • Display the "Theme Verse Poster" (item 4) on a focal wall.
  • Create a giant Bible verse word search on a dry erase board or a piece of poster board using a neutral colored marker such as black. (See pattern below Step 3.)

LIVE IT PREP
❑ *VBS 2023 Kids Activity Books*
❑ Bibles
❑ Pencils
❑ Dice

FINISH IT PREP
❑ *VBS 2023 Memory Maker* and Day 5 tags
❑ Yellow cardstock
❑ 2-inch circle punch
❑ Pens
  • Punch circles out of cardstock (1 per kid).

KNOW IT (6 MINUTES)

1. Group the kids into two teams and give each team a different color of marker. Have the teams line up across the room from the word search.

2. Explain that teams will take turns sending a player to the puzzle. The player will have five seconds to stand in front of the puzzle and locate and circle one word of the Bible verse. Players should locate verse words in order. If they can't find the next word in time, they run back to their team, and the other team takes a turn. Request a leader to stand near the word search to help keep score and help kids know what words they're looking for if needed.

3. Congratulate the team that circles the most Bible verse words as the winner.

CSB:

```
H  J  M  J  H  I  S  M  Y
P  O  E  V  C  Q  D  A  I
S  Y  D  Y  A  L  U  K  S
G  H  O  O  E  Y  D  E  H
X  U  O  U  T  O  J  O  T
R  Y  L  R  S  Y  A  W  A
L  O  R  D  R  C  T  K  P
L  I  M  E  R  E  Z  T  O
S  K  N  O  W  N  P  A  V
```

KJV:

```
E  X  M  S  T  E  A  C  H
T  T  H  E  C  Y  P  K  A
H  E  B  Y  P  D  H  B  Z
W  P  H  A  H  O  U  R  A
B  S  T  P  S  T  G  S  Y
Y  H  Z  X  Y  O  T  V  D
S  S  B  U  A  E  X  R  T
B  Z  E  M  W  D  O  D  H
V  E  J  K  K  L  U  Y  Y
```

LIVE IT (6 MINUTES)

1. Give the kids their activity books, Bibles, and pencils. Lead them to open their books to page 12.

2. Ask: "What did God teach Peter through the vision He gave him?" *(Jesus is for everyone.)*

3. Say: "It turns out that Jesus wants people all over the world to know who He is! He wants everyone to be saved and to have a relationship with Him! We are going to talk about what people in a few different places need to know about Jesus."

4. Guide the kids to find the activity on page 13.

5. You can give each child a die or roll one for the whole group to help choose which location to solve first. Work together to complete the activity.

FINISH IT (2 MINUTES)

1. Give kids the Day 5 tags to add to their Memory Makers.

2. Ask them to think about people they know who might not realize that Jesus is for them too. Challenge them to tell someone this good news.

3. Distribute cardstock circles and allow kids to draw two different emoji faces, one on each side. Guide kids to add the emojis to their bags.

4. Say: "These faces can remind you to pray for people you know to believe in Jesus."

5. Pray for the kids, asking God to help them remember things that they've learned about Jesus in VBS this week and to be with them through the twists and turns of their lives.

ROLL-A-MEEPLE

(Application Activity #1—10 minutes)

- ❑ Pack item 26
- ❑ Dice
- ❑ Paper
- ❑ Pencils, markers, or crayons
- • Copy "Roll-a-Meeple" (item 26) (1 copy for every 2 kids).

1. Group the kids into pairs and give each pair two sheets of paper, a die, and a copy of "Roll-a-Meeple" (item 26).

2. Say: "Does anyone know what a 'meeple' is? It's a small, person-shaped game piece that people use to move across a gameboard. We're going to create our own meeples, but we don't get to make the choices! We're going to roll the dice to see which shapes we get to use to create our meeples."

3. Guide kids to take turns rolling the dice and drawing the facial feature that corresponds with the turn they're on and the number they rolled. After six turns each, both kids should have completed faces for their meeples.

4. Guide kids to share the faces they drew with the group. Remind kids that just like they didn't get to choose the facial features of their meeples, we don't get to choose who is worthy of receiving Jesus' love. God showed Peter in his vision that Jesus is for everyone! We need to be prepared to tell the people we meet that Jesus loves them and can offer them forgiveness and a relationship with Him.

Item 26

REVIEW STACK-O

(Application Activity #2—10 minutes)

- ❑ Pack items 3, 10, 14, 21, and 25
- ❑ Masking tape
- ❑ Permanent marker
- ❑ Jenga® type blocks
- • Gather all 5 Bible story pictures (items 3, 10, 14, 21, and 25).
- • Place strips of tape on the blocks to provide a writing surface. Write two numbers on each block: one number corresponding to a day of Bible study and one to a review question from that day's Bible story picture (items 3, 10, 14, 21, and 25). So 1.4 would be Day 1, Question 4 and 4.5 would be Day 4, Question 5. You will have leftover blocks. Feel free to repeat some questions and leave some blocks blank. For fun, you could make a sixth list of silly questions to add to some of the blocks, like "What's your favorite kind of soup?" or "If you had a pet lizard what would you name it?"
- ❑ Lay three blocks side by side. Stack a second layer of blocks at a 90 degree angle to the first layer. Continue alternating layers, using all blocks.

1. Play, allowing kids to take turns pulling out blocks. If they pull out a block with numbers on it, they must answer the corresponding question.

2. Encourage kids to get help from the group if they don't remember the answer.

3. Continue playing. If the tower falls, set it up again and continue as time allows.

TINY TWISTED BIBLE GAME

(Bible Skills Activity—10 minutes)

❑ Pack items 12, 27, and 28

❑ Brads

❑ Paper clips

• Place a paper clip in the center of each spinner, attaching it loosely with a brad.

• Display the "Books of the Bible Poster" (item 12).

• Cut apart the "Tiny Twisted Bible Cards and Spinners" (items 27 and 28).

1. Group the kids into pairs or small groups and give each a "Tiny Twisted Bible Card" (item 27) and a "Tiny Twisted Bible Spinner" (item 28).

2. Explain that the kids are going to play a game using some of the divisions in the Bible. Point out that they may need to refer to the "Books of the Bible Poster" (item 12) for help.

3. Say: "Bible books are placed in different categories or divisions depending on what kind of books they are."

4. Explain that each card contains a few divisions. These are:
   • History *(books that record historical events)*
   • Prophets *(books in which God sent messages directly to His people)*
   • Letters *(letters church leaders like Peter wrote to different churches to teach them)*
   • Gospels *(books about the life, death, and resurrection of Jesus)*

5. Allow kids to take turns spinning and playing the game. If someone lands on "Prophets" in the "Pinky" quadrant of the spinner, he will need to touch a prophet on the card with his pinky finger. He will have to leave his pinky finger in this position until he spins the pinky quadrant again.

6. Play continues, placing more fingers on more colors. Eventually, someone's fingers will become too twisted to continue. Play several rounds as time allows.

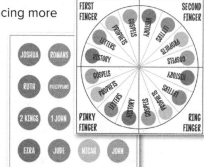

Items 27 & 28

POP SCOTCH

(Bonus Verse Activity—10 minutes)

❑ Pack item 29

❑ Black marker

❑ Tape

❑ Paper

❑ Roll of air bubble packaging

• Before the session, write the words of Acts 10:43 on white paper with a black marker, one word per page. Lay the pages out on the floor in word order like a hopscotch board.

• Place the packaging on top of the words. Use tape to secure the paper and wrap to the floor.

• Display the "Day 5 Bonus Verse Poster: Acts 10:43" (item 29).

1. Guide kids to sit on the opposite side of the room from the hopscotch board you created.

2. Read the "Day 5 Bonus Verse Poster: Acts 10:43" (item 29) together.

3. Say: "Did you know that hundreds of years before Jesus was ever born, prophets wrote about Him? They wrote about His birth, His life, and His death. The prophets knew these things about Jesus because God revealed messages to them. These prophecies help prove that Jesus is who He said He is: the One sent by God to save us from our sins!"

4. Let the kids take turns hopping on the words in order, saying the verse aloud and popping the wrap as they go.

5. Peel up wrap periodically and replace a word from the verse with blank paper. Guide kids to continue jumping and saying the verse, including the words that are missing.

EVERYDAY SUPPLIES

(These items needed every day in VBS are only listed here and do not appear in each day's specific supply listing.)

- ❏ Bibles
- ❏ *VBS 2023 Kids Activity Books* (9781087772080)
- ❏ *VBS 2023 Grades 3–4 Bible Study Leader Pack* (9781087771724), including the Music for Kids CD found in the pack
- ❏ *VBS 2023 Memory Maker* (9781087776545)
- ❏ Music device
- ❏ Pencils, pens, crayons, and markers (washable and permanent)
- ❏ Glue and tape (masking, painter's, and duct)
- ❏ Scissors
- ❏ Paper
- ❏ Basket for holding Memory Makers each day

DAY 1

- ❏ Pack items 1–9
- ❏ Various game pieces
- ❏ Paper sack
- ❏ Colored paper
- ❏ Clear contact plastic
- ❏ *VBS 2023 Giant Inflatable Game Cube* (9781087779812)
- ❏ Plastic box
- ❏ Large fish stuffed animal
- ❏ **Jesus Equals Perfection** (*Application Activity #1*)
  - Paper clips
  - Timer
- ❏ **Fishing for People** (*Application Activity #2*)
  - No supplies needed
- ❏ **New Testament Connection** (*Bible Skills Activity*)
  - Sticky notes in two colors (1½ by 2 inches or similar)
- ❏ **Fish Finder** (*Bonus Verse Activity*)
  - No additional supplies needed

DAY 2

- ❏ Pack items 1, 2, 4, and 10–13
- ❏ Timer
- ❏ Water
- ❏ Plastic storage tub
- ❏ Small pieces of corkboard or pool noodle
- ❏ 3–4 items of different sizes, weights, and shapes that will sink in the water
- ❏ Chenille stems
- ❏ Paper towels
- ❏ Gameboard path from Day 1 "Start It"
- ❏ Small basket
- ❏ Small stones or other simple objects that will sink
- ❏ Gallon-sized ziplock bags
- ❏ Blue food color
- ❏ Foam sheets
- ❏ **When Can I Trust Jesus?** (*Application Activity #1*)
  - Paper clips
  - Brads
  - Cardstock
- ❏ **Get Out of the Boat** (*Application Activity #2*)
  - Dry erase board and markers (optional)
- ❏ **On a Roll** (*Bible Skills Activity*)
  - *VBS 2023 Giant Inflatable Game Cubes* (2) (9781087779812) or 2 square boxes
- ❏ **Tic-tac-verse-know** (*Bonus Verse Activity*)
  - Dry erase board, marker, and eraser

DAY 3

- ☐ Pack items 1, 2, 4, 12, and 14–19
- ☐ Rubber chicken
- ☐ Resistance band (or similar stretchy item)
- ☐ Plastic cups
- ☐ Table
- ☐ Small ziplock bag
- ☐ Fish-shaped crackers
- ☐ Glass jar with a lid
- ☐ Vegetable oil
- ☐ Water
- ☐ Blue food color
- ☐ Balloons
- ☐ Allergy Alert
- ☐ Feathers (optional)
- ☐ Straight pin
- ☐ **A Day in the Life** (Application Activity #1)
  - Dice
  - Small stones or pennies (1 per kid)
- ☐ **Quick Draw** (Application Activity #2)
  - Dry erase board, markers, and eraser
  - Cup
  - Timer
- ☐ **Ready to Roll** (Bible Skills Activity)
  - Dice (1 for every 2 kids)
- ☐ **The Bible Verse Effect** (Bonus Verse Activity)
  - Dominoes

DAY 4

- ☐ Pack items 1, 2, 4, 12, and 20–23
- ☐ Flashlight and batteries
- ☐ Gameboard path from Day 1 "Start It"
- ☐ Small flashlights (1 per kid)
- ☐ Paper plates
- ☐ 6 beanbags
- ☐ Yellow cardstock
- ☐ **Ups and Downs** (Application Activity #1)
  - Dice (1 per group of 2–3 kids)
  - Small stones
- ☐ **Chitter Chatter** (Application Activity #2)
  - No additional supplies needed
- ☐ **The Last Shall Be First** (Bible Skills Activity)
  - Index cards
- ☐ **Just Guess** (Bonus Verse Activity)
  - Chairs (1 per kid)

DAY 5

- ☐ Pack items 1–4, 10, 12, 14, 21, and 24–29
- ☐ 3 small balls with emoji faces
- ☐ Small bag
- ☐ Circle stickers
- ☐ Timer
- ☐ Dry erase board and markers or poster board and permanent markers (3 colors of marker)
- ☐ Dice
- ☐ Yellow cardstock
- ☐ 2-inch circle punch
- ☐ **Roll-a-Meeple** (Application Activity #1)
  - Dice
- ☐ **Review Stack-O** (Application Activity #2)
  - Jenga® type blocks
- ☐ **Tiny Twisted Bible Game** (Bible Skills Activity)
  - Brads
  - Paper clips
- ☐ **Pop Scotch** (Bonus Verse Activity)
  - Roll of air bubble packaging